Collected Poems

COLLECTED POEMS

1928-1953

STEPHEN SPENDER

RANDOM HOUSE

NEW YORK

DESIGN: Marshall Lee

To Natasha

CONTENTS

Introduction : xv

PART ONE 1930–1933

PRELUDES

1 He will watch the hawk with an indifferent eye : 3
2 Rolled over on Europe: the sharp dew frozen to stars : 4
3 Marston, dropping it in the grate, broke his pipe : 5
4 Not to you I sighed. No, not a word : 6
5 Acts passed beyond the boundary of mere wishing : 7
6 At the end of two months' holiday there came a night : 8
7 Different living is not living in different places : 9
8 An 'I' can never be great man : 10
9 Beethoven's Death Mask : 11
10 Never being, but always at the edge of Being : 13
11 My parents kept me from children who were rough : 14
12 What I expected, was : 15
13 In 1929 : 17
14 The Port : 19
15 Moving through the silent crowd : 20
16 Who live under the shadow of a war : 21
17 Shapes of death haunt life : 22
18 How strangely this sun reminds me of my love : 24
19 To T.A.R.H. : 25
20 The Prisoners : 26
21 Without that once clear aim, the path of flight : 28
22 Passing, men are sorry for the birds in cages : 29

23 Oh young men, oh young comrades : 31
24 I think continually of those who were truly great : 32
25 Your body is stars whose million glitter here : 33
26 After they have tired of the brilliance of cities : 34
27 Perhaps : 36
28 The Funeral : 38
29 The Express : 39
30 The Landscape near an Aerodrome : 41
31 The Pylons : 43
32 In railway halls, on pavements near the traffic : 44
33 Abrupt and charming mover : 45
34 From all these events, from the slump, from the war,
    from the boom : 47
35 Not palaces, an era's crown : 49

PART TWO   1933–1939

A HEAVEN-PRINTED WORLD

Polar Exploration : 53
The Living Values : 55
The Uncreating Chaos : 57
Exiles from Their Land, History Their Domicile : 61
An Elementary School Classroom in a Slum : 64
A Footnote *From Marx's Chapter,* The Working Day : 66
Hoelderlin's Old Age : 68

PART THREE   1933–1939

OBSESSIONS

Variations on My Life : 71
Archaic Head : 75
Dark and Light : 76

PART FOUR   1936–1939

POEMS ABOUT THE SPANISH CIVIL WAR

The Room Above the Square : 81
Thoughts During an Air Raid : 82
Two Armies : 83
Ultima Ratio Regum : 85
A Stopwatch and an Ordnance Map : 87
In No Man's Land : 88
The Coward : 89
Fall of a City : 91
Port Bou : 93
To a Spanish Poet : 95

PART FIVE   1937–1939

LOVE AND SEPARATION

Two Kisses : 99
The Little Coat : 100
The Vase of Tears : 102
Song : 103
No Orpheus No Eurydice : 105
The Double Shame : 107
Auf Dem Wasser zu Singen : 109
A Separation : 111

PART SIX   1940–1944

POEMS ABOUT WAR

The War God : 115
Air Raid Across the Bay at Plymouth : 117
June 1940 : 119
The Drowned : 122

Rejoice in the Abyss : 124
A Man-Made World : 126
Memento : 128
The Fates : 129
Epilogue to a Human Drama : 134

PART SEVEN   1944

EXPLORATIONS

We fly through a night of stars : 139
I. Within our nakedness, nakedness still : 139
II. Were born; must die; were loved; must love : 140
III. Since we are what we are, what shall we be : 140
IV. Exiles from single Being of Belief : 141
V. The Immortal Spirit is that single ghost : 141
VI. One is the witness through whom the whole : 142

PART EIGHT   1945

ELEGY FOR MARGARET

I. Darling of our hearts, drowning : 145
II. From a tree choked by ivy, rotted : 146
III. Poor girl, inhabitant of a stark land : 148
IV. Already you are beginning to become : 149
V. The final act of love : 150
VI. Dearest and nearest brother : 152

PART NINE   1941–1949

MEETINGS AND ABSENCE

The Dream : 157
One : 158
Absence : 159

Daybreak : 160
Lost : 161
Seascape : 163
The Barn : 165
Dusk : 167
Meeting : 170
Ice : 173
Word : 174
The Trance : 175
O : 177

PART TEN   1950–1953

LATER POEMS

In Attica : 181
Messenger : 182
Empty House : 185
To My Daughter : 186
Missing My Daughter : 187
Nocturne : 189
Sirmione Peninsula : 192
Dylan Thomas (November 1953) : 194

PART ELEVEN   1928–1929

EARLY POEMS

The Cries of Evening : 197
The Swan : 198
That Girl Who Laughed : 199
Lying Awake : 200

1935

After Rilke: Orpheus Eurydice Hermes : 201

INTRODUCTION

To collect and select these poems, I copied them into a large note-book, then typed them out and tried to consider how each poem would best take its place in a single volume. In this way, I have spent several months reconsidering and even re-experiencing poems I have written over the past twenty-five years.

Now that I end this work with writing its beginning, I can see that my aim has been to retrieve as many past mistakes, and to make as many improvements, as possible, without 'cheating.' The awareness of the danger of 'cheating' implies a consciousness of obligations: obligations to the reader, and, more important, obligations to remain true to the felt experiences from which the poems, when they were first written, arose. Poetry is a game played with the reader according to rules, but it is also a truth game in which the truth is outside the rules.

There seemed to me several practical obligations to the reader which should be observed. One was to put in poems which, because they had already appeared in anthologies, he would reasonably feel entitled to expect in a collected volume. To this extent I had to consider his anticipation as well as my own judgment. Next, there seemed an obligation to 'own up' to those poems, like *The Pylons* and *The Funeral,* which, when they were written, provided a particular label for some of the poetry of the 'Thirties: an embarrassment to my friends' luggage more even than to my own. It would perhaps be excusable to disclaim these give-aways now; yet when I come to look at them, they seem to me better than many of the poems I have thrown overboard. In any case, they have a slight historic interest which, I feel, ought to be represented. Another reason for including them might be that since they are here, the reader can see how uncharacteristic they are of most of these poems.

Another obligation was to stick roughly to the 'order in which the poems were written.' All the same, I have, I think, improved this order, by relating it to the autobiographical development behind the poetry, instead of merely approximating it to a timetable of dates when each poem was completed.

Having put the poems into this autobiographical order, I found that those in the volume *Poems* (1933) formed a solid block in which I had made very few internal changes, and none of which stepped out of its volume. This was not so with those in the other volumes, which broke down the contours of their original publication in order to form such groupings as: poems about the Spanish Civil War; poems of love and separation; some very introspective poems; the poems written on war-time England; the group of poems with which Part Two of this volume opens (these are really attempts to write Odes); and so on.

Another obligation was not to alter drastically those poems which are, I think, fairly well known: poems which, partly just because I feel they are known, seem to have passed out of my hands beyond recall. But there are, in my published volumes, several less known poems which have remained, as it were, still malleable. One of these is *Exiles from Their Land, History Their Domicile*, a poem about those who have, after their deaths, obtained for their lives a symbolic significance which certainly passed unnoticed when they were living. The important (to me) subject of this poem is the legend of their unity of being which such exiles have imposed on the imaginations of those who come after them. It seems to me that the expression of an idea of this kind may never seem satisfactory to a poet and the effort to achieve it may preoccupy him for many years. If he feels he has failed to interpret it in one version he can re-invent it, because he does not ever forget the complete intention behind the incomplete failure. The poems that I have most re-worked here are those about obsessive themes that are always with me.

A temptation I have guarded against is that of making more than a discreet and almost unnoticeable minimum of technical tidyings up. Nothing seems easier when one is older, than to correct a rhyme or rhythm which eluded one's youthful incompetence. Yet the technical flaw in an early poem may reflect a true inadequacy to impose a finished form upon an incomplete experience. It may even (as in the juvenilia of most good poets) have a certain beauty in realizing the rightness of such an incompleteness. A correction may therefore have the result of turning something which had the rough quality of a flaw in a semiprecious stone, into a work of superficial preciosity.

Another form of rewriting I have avoided is any attempt to remove inconsistencies of idea or feeling, or to bring the beliefs expressed in the early poems into line with my later ideas.

What I would hope of this volume is that it is a weeded, though not a tidied up or altered garden. The faults and flaws are there, but I hope they are more solid and apparent, and less vague and confused. I hope there are fewer muddles and irrelevancies, and a greater simplicity. I hope that anyone who has the patience to read through all the volume will see certain broad lines of development more clearly and strongly expressed than he might have expected from reading twice as many poems in the previously published volumes. But in this hope I may well be deluded, for with poetry one is less sure than with anything else.

30th May, 1954

PART ONE

1930–1933

PRELUDES

To Christopher Isherwood

He will watch the hawk with an indifferent eye
       Or pitifully;
Nor on those eagles that so feared him, now
       Will strain his brow;
Weapons men use, stone, sling and strong-thewed bow
       He will not know.
This aristocrat, superb of all instinct,
       With death close linked
Had paced the enormous cloud, almost had won
       War on the sun;
Till now, like Icarus mid-ocean-drowned,
       Hands, wings, are found.

Rolled over on Europe: the sharp dew frozen to stars
Below us; above our heads, the night
Frozen again to stars; the stars
In pools between our coats; and that charmed moon.
Ah, what supports? What cross draws out our arms,
Heaves up our bodies towards the wind
And hammers us between the mirrored lights?

Only my body is real; which wolves
Are free to oppress and gnaw. Only this rose
My friend laid on my breast, and these few lines
Written from home, are real.

Marston, dropping it in the grate, broke his pipe.
Nothing hung on this act, it was no symbol
Ludicrous for calamity, but merely ludicrous.

That heavy-wrought briar with the great pine face
Now split across like a boxer's hanging dream
Of punishing a nigger, he brought from the continent;
It was his absurd relic, like bones,
Of stamping on the white face mountains,
Early beds in huts, and other journeys.

To hold the banks of the Danube, the slow barges down the
          river,
Those coracles with faces painted on,
Demanded his last money,
A foodless journey home, as pilgrimage.

4

Not to you I sighed. No, not a word.
We climbed together. Any feeling was
Formed with the hills. It was like trees' unheard
And monumental sign of country peace.

But next day, stumbling, panting up dark stairs,
Rushing in room and door flung wide, I knew.
Oh empty walls, book-carcases, blank chairs
All splintered in my head and cried for you.

Acts passed beyond the boundary of mere wishing
Not privy looks, hedged words, at times you saw.
These, blundering, heart-surrendered troopers were
Small presents made, and waiting for the tram.
Then once you said: 'Waiting was very kind',
And looked surprised. Surprising for me, too,
Whose every movement had been missionary,
A pleading tongue unheard. I had not thought
That you, who nothing else saw, would see this.

So 'very kind' was merest overflow
Something I had not reckoned in myself,
A chance deserter from my force. When we touched hands,
I felt the whole rebel, feared mutiny
And turned away,
Thinking, if these were tricklings through a dam,
I must have love enough to run a factory on,
Or give a city power, or drive a train.

At the end of two months' holiday there came a night
When I lay awake and the seas' distant fretless scansion
By imagination scourged rose to a fight
Like the town's roar, pouring forth apprehension.
I was on a train. Like the quick spool of a film
I watched hasten away the simple green which can heal
Sadness. The signpost painted FERRY TO WILM
And the cottage by the lake shone, vivid, but unreal.

      Real were iron rails, and, smashing the grass,
Real these wheels on which I rode, real this compelled time.
Unreal those cows, those wave-winged storks, that lime
Painted on enamel behind the moving glass.
      Those burned in a clear world from which we pass
Like ROSE and LOVE in a forgotten rhyme.

Different living is not living in different places
But creating in the mind a map
And willing on that map a desert
Pinnacled mountain, or saving resort.

When I frowned, making desert, Time only
Shook once his notchless column, as when **Ape**
Centuries before, with furrowed hand
Fumbled at stone, discerning new use:
Setting his mark against mind's progress;
Shaking Time, but with no change of Place.

An 'I' can never be great man.
This known great one has weakness
To friends is most remarkable for weakness:
His ill-temper at meals, dislike of being contradicted,
His only real pleasure fishing in ponds,
His only real wish—forgetting.

To advance from friends to the composite self,
Central 'I' is surrounded by 'I eating',
'I loving', 'I angry', 'I excreting',
And the great 'I' planted in him
Has nothing to do with all these,

Can never claim its true place
Resting in the forehead, and calm in his gaze.
The great 'I' is an unfortunate intruder
Quarrelling with 'I tiring' and 'I sleeping'
And all those other 'I's who long for 'We dying'.

BEETHOVEN'S DEATH MASK

I imagine him still with heavy brow.
Huge, black, with bent head and falling hair,
He ploughs the landscape. His face
Is this hanging mask transfigured,
This mask of death which the white lights make stare.

I see the thick hands clasped; the scare-crow coat;
The light strike upwards at the holes for eyes;
The beast squat in that mouth, whose opening is
The hollow opening of an organ pipe:
There the wind sings and the harsh longing cries.

He moves across my vision like a ship.
What else is iron but he? The fields divide
And, heaving, are changing waters of the sea.
He is prisoned, masked, shut off from Being.
Life, like a fountain, he sees leap—outside.

Yet, in that head there twists the roaring cloud
And coils, as in a shell, the roaring wave.
The damp leaves whisper; bending to the rain
The April rises in him, chokes his lungs
And climbs the torturing passage of his brain.

Then the drums move away, the Distance shows:
Now cloud-hid peaks are bared; the mystic One
Horizons haze, as the blue incense, heaven.
Peace, paece. . . . Then splitting skull and dream, there comes
Blotting our lights, the Trumpeter, the sun.

Never being, but always at the edge of Being,
My head—Death Mask—is brought into the sun.
With shadow pointing finger across cheek,
I move lips for tasting, I move hands for touching,
But never come nearer than touching
Though Spirit lean outward for seeing.
Observing rose, gold, eyes, an admired landscape,
My senses record the act of wishing,
Wishing to be
Rose, gold, landscape or another.
I claim fulfilment in the fact of loving.

My parents kept me from children who were rough
Who threw words like stones and who wore torn clothes.
Their thighs showed through rags. They ran in the street
And climbed cliffs and stripped by the country streams.

I feared more than tigers their muscles like iron
Their jerking hands and their knees tight on my arms.
I feared the salt coarse pointing of those boys
Who copied my lisp behind me on the road.

They were lithe, they sprang out behind hedges
Like dogs to bark at my world. They threw mud
While I looked the other way, pretending to smile.
I longed to forgive them, but they never smiled.

What I expected, was
Thunder, fighting,
Long struggles with men
And climbing.
After continual straining
I should grow strong;
Then the rocks would shake,
And I rest long.

What I had not foreseen
Was the gradual day
Weakening the will
Leaking the brightness away,
The lack of good to touch,
The fading of body and soul
—Smoke before wind,
Corrupt, unsubstantial.

The wearing of Time,
And the watching of cripples pass
With limbs shaped like questions
In their odd twist,

The pulverous grief
Melting the bones with pity,
The sick falling from earth—
These, I could not foresee.

Expecting always
Some brightness to hold in trust,
Some final innocence
Exempt from dust,
That, hanging solid,
Would dangle through all,
Like the created poem,
Or faceted crystal.

13

A whim of Time, the general arbiter,
Proclaims the love, instead of death, of friends.
Under the domed sky and athletic sun
Three stand naked: the new, bronzed German,
The communist clerk, and myself, being English.

Yet to unwind the travelled sphere twelve years
Then two take arms, spring to a ghostly posture.
Or else roll on the thing a further ten
And this poor clerk with world-offended eyes
Builds with red hands his heaven; makes our bones
The necessary scaffolding to peace.

    •   •   •

Now I suppose that the once-envious dead
Have learned a strict philosophy of clay
After these centuries, to haunt us no longer
In the churchyard or at the end of the lane
Or howling at the edge of the city
Beyond the last beanrows, near the new factory.

Our fathers killed. And yet there lives no feud
Like Hamlet prompted on the castle stair;
There falls no shade across our blank of peace
We being together, struck across our path,
Nor taper finger threatening solitude.

Our fathers' misery, the ghost's mercy,
The cynic's mystery, weave this philosophy:
That the history of man, traced purely from dust,
Is lipping skulls on the revolving rim
Or posture of genius with the granite head bowed:

Lives risen a moment, joined or separate,
Fall heavily, then are always separate,
Stratum unreckoned by geologists,
Sod lifted, turned, slapped back again with spade.

1 4

THE PORT

Hopelessly wound round with the cords of street
Men wander down their lines of level graves.
Sometimes the maze knots into flaring caves
Where magic-lantern faces tilt their greetings.
Smiles dawn with a harsh lightning, there's no speaking
And, far from lapping laughter, all's parched and hard.
Here the pale lily boys flaunt their bright lips,
Such pretty cups for money, and older whores
Scuttle rat-toothed into the dark outdoors.

Northwards, the sea exerts his huge mandate.
His guardians, candles stand, the furnace beam,
Blinking Pharos, and hammering from shipyards.
In their fat gardens, the merchants dwell, Southwards.
Well-lit, well-fed, well-spoken men are these,
With bronze-faced sons, and happy in their daughters.

Moving through the silent crowd
Who stand behind dull cigarettes,
These men who idle in the road,
I have the sense of falling light.

They lounge at corners of the street
And greet friends with a shrug of shoulder
And turn their empty pockets out,
The cynical gestures of the poor.

Now they've no work, like better men
Who sit at desks and take much pay
They sleep long nights and rise at ten
To watch the hours that drain away.

I'm jealous of the weeping hours
They stare through with such hungry eyes
I'm haunted by these images,
I'm haunted by their emptiness.

Who live under the shadow of a war,
What can I do that matters?
My pen stops, and my laughter, dancing, stop,
Or ride to a gap.

How often, on the powerful crest of pride,
I am shot with thought
That halts the untamed horses of the blood,
The grip on good;

That moving, whimpering, and mating, bear
Tunes to deaf ears:
Stuffed with the realer passions of the earth
Beneath this hearth.

Shapes of death haunt life.
What each most wills, projects his place beyond.
Unrequited love, never solving
The need to become another's body
Yearns toward dissolution.
The greed for property
Heaps a skyscraper over the breathing ribs.
The speed-lines of dictators
Cut their own stalks.
From afar, we watch the best of us—
Whose adored desire was to die into all Time.

Ambition is my wish: that flat thin flame
I feed, plants my own shadow. It changes love
For love of being loved, or loving.
The humorous day-contented drunkenness
Abjures, demands that marble monuments
Be built on words. Yet who can stop
His death-will's industry, which even in sleep
Mass-produces tombs? And buries under indolence
Earthquakes, and new births of death?

And yet the swallows by autumnal instinct
Comfort us in their effortless exhaustion

In wide unguided flight to their complete South.
There, above timeless pyramids, they perch,
Simply for delight, their one compulsion.
Not teaching us to love, yet soothing our gaze:
Not saving me from death, yet loosening me for speech.

How strangely this sun reminds me of my love!
Of my walk alone at evening, when like the cottage smoke
Hope vanished into the red fading of the sky.
I remember my strained listening to his voice
My staring at his face and taking the photograph
With the river behind, and the woods touched by Spring:
Till the identification of a morning—
Expansive sheets of blue rising from fields
Roaring movements of light discerned under shadow—
With his figure leaning over a map, is now complete.

What is left of that smoke which the wind blew away?
I corrupted his confidence and his sun-like happiness
So that even now in his turning of bolts or driving a machine
His hand will show error. That is for him.
For me this memory which now I behold,
When, from the pasturage, azure rounds me in rings,
And the lark ascends, and his voice still rings, still rings.

T O T . A . R . H .

Even whilst I watch him I am remembering
The quick laugh of the wasp-gold eyes.
The statue turning from the staring window
Even while I see I remember, for love
Dips what it sees into a flood of memory
Vaster than itself, and makes the seen
Be drowned in all that past and future seeing
Of the once seen. Thus what I wore I wear
And shall wear always—the glint of the quick lids
And the body's axle turning: these shall be
      What they are now within the might of Ever.

Night when my life lies with no past or future
But only endless space. It wakes and watches
Hope and despair and the small vivid longings
Gnaw the flesh, like minnows. Where it drank love
It breathes in sameness. Here are
The signs indelible. The wiry copper hair,
And the notched mothlike lips, and that after all human
Glance, which makes all else forgiven.

THE PRISONERS

Far far the least of all, in want,
Are these,
The prisoners
Turned massive with their vaults and dark with dark.

They raise no hands, which rest upon their knees,
But lean their solid eyes against the night,
Dimly they feel
Only the furniture they use in cells.

Their Time is almost Death. The silted flow
Of years on years
Is marked by dawns
As faint as cracks on mud-flats of despair.

My pity moves amongst them like a breeze
On walls of stone,
Fretting for summer leaves, or like a tune
On ears of stone.

Then, when I raise my hands to strike,
It is too late,
There are no chains that fall
Nor visionary liquid door
Melted with anger.

When have their lives been free from walls and dark
And airs that choke?
And where less prisoner, to let my anger
Like a sun strike?

If I could follow them from room to womb
To plant some hope
Through the black silk of the big-bellied gown,
There would I win.

No, no, no,
It is too late for anger,
Nothing prevails
But pity for the grief they cannot feel.

Without that once clear aim, the path of flight
To follow for a lifetime through white air,
This century chokes me under roots of night.
I suffer like history in Dark Ages, where
Truth lies in dungeons, too deep for whisper.
We hear of towers long broken off from sight
And tortures and wars, smoky and dark with rumour,
But on Mind's buried thought there falls no light.
Watch me who walk through coiling streets where rain
And fog choke every sigh; round corners of day,
Road-drills explore new areas of pain,
Nor trees reach leaf-lit branches down to play.
The city climbs in horror to my brain,
The writings are my only wings away.

Passing, men are sorry for the birds in cages
And for unrestricted nature, hedged and lined.
But what do they say to your pleasant bird
Physical dalliance, since years confined?

Behind three centuries, behind the trimmed park,
Woods you felled, your clothes, houses you built,
Only love remembers where that bird dipped his head,
Only suns, light-years distant, flash along his neck.

Dance will you, and sing? Yet swear he is dead.
Invent politics to hide him and law suits and suits.
Now he's forbidden, and quite banned like grass,
Where the fields are covered with suburban houses.

I never hear you are 'happy' but I wonder
Whether this was at a bazaar or in a car,
At a dance or a party, that you could create
Procrastination of love, for your talk and laughter are
A glass that flashes back cold light
And that offers only hate.

Will you not forgive him? I've signed his release
Thrilling and gentle as the pulse's drum
His curvetting joy wakes the solitary stag
From his coveted sleep.

Yes! And if you still bar your pretty bird, remember
Revenge and despair make their home in your bowels.
Life cannot pardon a purity without scruple
The knife in one's own flesh, the angel and destroyer,
Inventor of self-martyrdom, serene and terrible.

Oh young men, oh young comrades
it is too late now to stay in those houses
your fathers built where they built you to breed
money on money   it is too late
to make or even to count what has been made
Count rather those fabulous possessions
which begin with your body and your fiery soul:
the hairs on your head the muscles extending
in ranges with lakes across your limbs
Count your eyes as jewels and your valued sex
then count the sun and the innumerable coined light
sparkling on waves and spangling under trees
It is too late now to stay in great houses where the ghosts are
        prisoned
—those ladies like flies perfect in amber
those financiers like fossils of bones in coal.
Oh comrades, step beautifully from the solid wall
advance to rebuild and sleep with friend on hill
advance to rebel and remember what you have
no ghost ever had, immured in his hall.

I think continually of those who were truly great.
Who, from the womb, remembered the soul's history
Through corridors of light where the hours are suns,
Endless and singing. Whose lovely ambition
Was that their lips, still touched with fire,
Should tell of the Spirit, clothed from head to foot in song.
And who hoarded from the Spring branches
The desires falling across their bodies like blossoms.

What is precious, is never to forget
The essential delight of the blood drawn from ageless springs
Breaking through rocks in worlds before our earth.
Never to deny its pleasure in the morning simple light
Nor its grave evening demand for love.
Never to allow gradually the traffic to smother
With noise and fog, the flowering of the Spirit.

Near the snow, near the sun, in the highest fields,
See how these names are fêted by the waving grass
And by the streamers of white cloud
And whispers of wind in the listening sky.
The names of those who in their lives fought for life,
Who wore at their hearts the fire's centre.
Born of the sun, they travelled a short while toward the sun,
And left the vivid air signed with their honour.

Your body is stars whose million glitter here:
I am lost among the branches of this sky
Here near my breast, here in my nostrils, here
Where our vast arms like streams of fire lie.

How can this end? My healing fills the night
And hangs its flags in worlds I cannot near.
Our movements range through miles, and when we kiss
The moment widens to enclose the years.

.   .   .

Beholders of the promised dawn of truth,
The explorers of immense and simple lines,
Here is our goal, men cried, but it was lost
Amongst the mountain mists and mountain pines.

So with this face of love, whose breathings are
A mystery shadowed on the desert floor:
The promise hangs, this swarm of stars and flowers,
And then there comes the shutting of a door.

After they have tired of the brilliance of cities
And of striving for office where at last they may languish
Hung round with easy chains until
Death and Jerusalem glorify also the crossing sweeper:
Then those streets the rich built and their easy love
Fade like old cloths, and it is death stalks through life
Grinning white through all faces
Clean and equal like the shine from snow.

In this day when grief pours freezing over us,
When the hard light of pain gleams at every street corner,
When those who were pillars of yesterday's roof
Shrink in their clothes: then surely from hunger
We may strike fire, like fire from flint?
And our strength is now the strength of our bones
Clean and equal like the shine from snow
And the strength of famine and our enforced idleness,
And it is the strength of our love for one another.

Readers of this strange language,
We have come at last to a country
Where light equal, like the shine from snow, strikes all faces.
Here you may wonder
How it was that works, money, interest, building, could ever
    hide
The palpable and obvious love of man for man.

Oh, comrades, let not those who follow after
—The beautiful generation that will spring from our sides—
Let them not wonder how after the failure of banks,
The failure of cathedrals and the declared insanity of our
        rulers,
We lacked the Spring-like resources of the tiger
Or of plants which strike out new roots to urgent waters.
Through torn-down portions of fabric let their eyes
Witness the admiring dawn explode like a shell
Around us, dazing us with its light like snow.

PERHAPS

The explosion of a bomb
The submarine—a burst bubble filled with water—
The Chancellor clutching his shot arm (and that was Perhaps
a put up job for their own photographers)
the parliament their own side set afire
and then Our Party banned
And the mine flooded—an accident, I hope.

motor-cycles wires aeroplanes cars trains
converging on that same town Geneva
top-hats talking at edge of silk-blue lake
then, the mountains.

We know things from rotating machines
from flanges stamping, cutting, unrolling sheets from rolls.
Newsmen are points of compass: their arms are
the four winds carrying printed legends.
Our eyes, fish wrapped in newspaper.

In his skidding car, the King wondered
watching the bayoneted landscape rush at him:
'Is it the enemy? (I cannot grasp it) or is it
at peace with its own peace I cannot touch?'

Was that final when they shot him? Did that war
lop off dead branches? Are the young men splendid?
Is it The Shape of Things to Come, that revolution
nosing whale-like at Antarctic edge?

Only Perhaps. Maybe that we grow smaller
donnish and bony, shut in our racing tombs:
these headlines are sides that shake and close
the dry dice rattled in their wooden box.

Maybe deception of things merely changing. Out there
Perhaps it is the dead above the plain
who grow; not our time bombs but Time
monstrous with stillness like that Alpine range.

THE FUNERAL

Death is another milestone on their way.
With laughter on their lips and with winds blowing round
            them
They record simply
How this one excelled all others in making driving belts.

This is festivity, it is the time of statistics,
When they record what one unit contributed:
They are glad as they lay him back in the earth
And thank him for what he gave them.

They walk home remembering the straining red flags,
And with pennons of song still fluttering through their blood
They speak of the World State
With its towns like brain centres and its pulsing arteries.

They think how one life hums, revolves and toils,
One cog in a golden singing hive:
Like spark from fire, its task happily achieved,
It falls away quietly.

No more are they haunted by the individual grief
Nor the crocodile tears of European genius,
The decline of a culture
Mourned by scholars who dream of the ghosts of Greek boys.

THE EXPRESS

After the first powerful, plain manifesto
The black statement of pistons, without more fuss
But gliding like a queen, she leaves the station.
Without bowing and with restrained unconcern
She passes the houses which humbly crowd outside,
The gasworks, and at last the heavy page
Of death, printed by gravestones in the cemetery.
Beyond the town, there lies the open country
Where, gathering speed, she acquires mystery,
The luminous self-possession of ships on ocean.
It is now she begins to sing—at first quite low
Then loud, and at last with a jazzy madness—
The song of her whistle screaming at curves,
Of deafening tunnels, brakes, innumerable bolts.
And always light, aerial, underneath,
Retreats the elate metre of her wheels.
Steaming through metal landscape on her lines,
She plunges new eras of white happiness,
Where speed throws up strange shapes, broad curves
And parallels clean like trajectories from guns.
At last, further than Edinburgh or Rome,
Beyond the crest of the world, she reaches night
Where only a low stream-line brightness
Of phosphorus on the tossing hills is light.

Ah, like a comet through flame, she moves entranced,
Wrapt in her music no bird song, no, nor bough
Breaking with honey buds, shall ever equal.

THE LANDSCAPE NEAR

AN AERODROME

More beautiful and soft than any moth
With burring furred antennae feeling its huge path
Through dusk, the air liner with shut-off engines
Glides over suburbs and the sleeves set trailing tall
To point the wind. Gently, broadly, she falls,
Scarcely disturbing charted currents of air.

Lulled by descent, the travellers across sea
And across feminine land indulging its easy limbs
In miles of softness, now let their eyes trained by watching
Penetrate through dusk the outskirts of this town
Here where industry shows a fraying edge.
Here they may see what is being done.

Beyond the winking masthead light
And the landing ground, they observe the outposts
Of work: chimneys like lank black fingers
Or figures, frightening and mad: and squat buildings
With their strange air behind trees, like women's faces
Shattered by grief. Here where few houses
Moan with faint light behind their blinds,
They remark the unhomely sense of complaint, like a dog
Shut out, and shivering at the foreign moon.

In the last sweep of love, they pass over fields
Behind the aerodrome, where boys play all day
Hacking dead grass: whose cries, like wild birds,
Settle upon the nearest roofs
But soon are hid under the loud city.

Then, as they land, they hear the tolling bell
Reaching across the landscape of hysteria,
To where, louder than all those batteries
And charcoaled towers against that dying sky,
Religion stands, the Church blocking the sun.

THE PYLONS

The secret of these hills was stone, and cottages
Of that stone made,
And crumbling roads
That turned on sudden hidden villages.

Now over these small hills, they have built the concrete
That trails black wire;
Pylons, those pillars
Bare like nude giant girls that have no secret.

The valley with its gilt and evening look
And the green chestnut
Of customary root,
Are mocked dry like the parched bed of a brook.

But far above and far as sight endures
Like whips of anger
With lightning's danger
There runs the quick perspective of the future.

This dwarfs our emerald country by its trek
So tall with prophecy:
Dreaming of cities
Where often clouds shall lean their swan-white neck.

In railway halls, on pavements near the traffic,
They beg, their eyes made big by empty staring
And only measuring Time, like the blank clock.

No, I shall wave no tracery of pen-ornament
To make them birds upon my singing-tree:
Time merely drives these lives which do not live
As tides push rotten stuff along the shore.

—There is no consolation, no, none,
In the curving beauty of that line
Traced on our graphs through History, where the oppressor
    Starves and deprives the poor.

Paint here no draped despairs, no saddening clouds
Where the soul rests, proclaims eternity.
But let the wrong cry out as raw as wounds
This time forgets and never heals, far less transcends.

Abrupt and charming mover,
Your pointed eyes under lit leaves,
Your light hair, your smile,
I watch burn in a foreign land
Bright through my dark night
And sheltered by my hand.

My nights are like a Jonah's whale
In which I dream you: from day
I have recalled your play
Disturbing as birds flying
And with the Spring's infection
And denial of satisfaction.

You dance, forgetting all: in joy
Sustaining that instant of the eye
Which like a Catherine wheel spins free.
Your games of cards, hockey with toughs,
Winking at girls, shoes cribbed from toffs,
Like the encircling summer dew
Glaze me from head to toe.

By night I hold you, and by day
I watch you weave the silk cocoon

Of a son's or a skater's play.
We have no meeting place
Beneath the brilliantine-bright surface.
The outward figure of delight
Creates your image that's no image
Dark in my dark language.

From all these events, from the slump, from the war, from
      the boom,
From the Italian holiday, from the skirring
Of the revolving light for one who fled,
From the crowds in the square at dusk, from the shooting,
From the loving, from the dying, however we prosper in death
Whether lying under twin lilies and branched candles
Or stiffened on the pavement like a frozen sack, hidden
From peace by the lamps:
From all these events, Time solitary will emerge
Like a rocket over mist: beyond the troubles,
Untangled with our pasts, be sure Time will leave us.

At first, growing up in us more nakedly than our own nature,
Driving us beyond what seemed the final choking swamp,
Ruin, the all-covering illness, to a new and empty air;
Singling us from the war that killed ten millions;
Bearing us elate through the cicada fields;
Nesting us in attics where our parents' voices
Floated up through windows from the night of gardens
Like water lilies on dark water;
Then sending us to lean days after the fulfilment;
Dropping us into the lunar crater of the dead.

Our universal ally, who cares not for our purpose, whose
          flanks
Stretch to planets unknown in our brief earth's battle,
Tomorrow Time will forget us even here,
When our bodies are rejected like the beetle's shard. Today
Already, now, we are forgotten on the stellar shores.
Time's ambition is all space, and hangs its flags
In night that never reaches us, years to which this world is
          dead.

Not palaces, an era's crown
Where the mind dwells, intrigues, rests;
Architectural gold-leaved flower
From people ordered like a single mind,
I build. This only what I tell:
It is too late for rare accumulation,
For family pride, for beauty's filtered dusts;
I say, stamping the words with emphasis,
Drink from here energy and only energy,
As from the electric charge of a battery,
To will this Time's change.
Eye, gazelle, delicate wanderer,
Drinker of horizon's fluid line;
Ear that suspends on a chord
The spirit drinking timelessness;
Touch, love, all senses;
Leave your gardens, your singing feasts,
Your dreams of suns circling before our sun,
Of heaven after our world.
Instead, watch images of flashing glass
That strike the outward sense, the polished will,
Flag of our purpose which the wind engraves.

No spirit seek here rest. But this: No one
Shall hunger: Man shall spend equally.

Our goal which we compel: Man shall be man.
          That programme of the antique Satan
Bristling with guns on the indented page,
With battleship towering from hilly waves:
For what? Drive of a ruining purpose
Destroying all but its age-long exploiters.
Our programme like this, but opposite,
Death to the killers, bringing light to life.

PART TWO

1933-1939

A HEAVEN-PRINTED WORLD

To Isaiah Berlin

Our single purpose was to walk through snow
With faces swung to their prodigious North
Like compass needles. As clerks in whited banks
Leave bird-claw pen-prints columned on white paper,
On snow we added footprints.
Extensive whiteness drowned
All sense of space. We tramped through
Static, glaring days, Time's suspended blank.
That was in Spring and Autumn. Summer struck
Water over rocks, and half the world
Became a ship with a deep keel, the booming floes
And icebergs with their little birds:
Twittering Snow Bunting, Greenland Wheatear,
Red-throated Divers; imagine butterflies,
Sulphurous cloudy yellow; burnish of bees
That suck from saxifrage; crowberry,
Bilberry, cranberry, *Pyrola Uniflora*.
There followed winter in a frozen hut
Warm enough at the kernel, but dare to sleep
With head against the wall—ice gummed my hair!
Hate Culver's loud breathing, despise Freeman's
Fidget for washing: love only the dogs
That whine for scraps, and scratch. Notice
How they run better (on short journeys) with a bitch.
In that, different from us.

Return, return, you warn! We do. There is
Your city, with railways, money, words, words, words.
Meals, papers, exchanges, debates,
Cinema, wireless: then there is Marriage.
I cannot sleep. At night I watch
A clear voice speak with words like drawing.
Its questions are white rifts:—Was
Ice, our rage transformed? The raw, the motionless
Skies, were these the Spirit's hunger?
The continual hypnotized march through snow,
The dropping nights of precious extinction, were these
Only the wide circuits of the will,
The frozen heart's evasions? If such thoughts seem
A kind of madness here, a coldness
Of snow like sheets in summer—is the North
Over there, a palpable, true madness,
A solid simplicity, absolute, without towns,
Only with bears and fish, a raging eye,
A new and singular sex?

THE LIVING VALUES

Alas for the sad standards
In the eyes of the Old Masters
Sprouting through glaze of their pictures!

Images we watch through glass
Look back on us, intruding on our time:
As Nature, spread before the summer mansion,
Butts through windows in on our dimension.

To airman over continental ranges,
Propellor's stiff and glassy flicker
Between him and the map below
Spells dynamics of this invisible
Age of invention, that whirls out of sight.

Varnish over paint, and dust over glass!
Stare back, remote, the drummer's static drum;
The locked ripeness of the Centaurs' feast;

The blowing flags, frozen stiff
Under cracked varnish, and the facing
Reproach of Rembrandt's self-Rembrandt.

Alas for the sad standards
In the eyes of the new-dead young
Sprawled in the mud of battle.
Stare back, stare back, with dust over glazed
Eyes, their gaze at partridges,
Their dreams of nudes, and their collected
Hearts wound up with love, like little watch springs.

To ram them outside Time, violence
Of wills that ride this cresting day
Struck them with lead so swift
They look at us through its glass trajectory
And we, living, look back at them through glass,
Their bodies now sunk inch-deep in gold frames.

Through the invisible they look at us,
Like values of Old Masters
That mock us with strange peace!

I

To the hanging despair of eyes in the street, offer
Your making hands, and your liver, on skewers of pity.
When the pyramid sky is built with clouds of sand which the
       yellow
Sun trumpets above, respond to that day's judgment
With a headache. Let your spirit follow
The young men to the Pole, up Everest, to war: by love, be
       shot.

For the uncreating chaos descends
And claims you in marriage: though a man you were ever a
       bride:
Ever beneath the supple surface of summery muscle,
The fountain evening talk cupping the stars,
The student who chucks back the lock of his hair in front of
       the glass
You were only anxious that your despair should last.

That engine in you, anxiety,
Was a grave lecher, globe-trotter, one
Whose moods were straws, the winds that bore them, aero-
       planes.
'Whatever happens, I shall never be alone,
I shall always have a fare, an affair, or a revolution.'

Without your buttressing gesture that yet so leans;
Is glad as a mat
When stamped on; blood that yearns to give suck to a
        vampire bat;
And heart fretted by storms like the rocks at Land's End;
Without some mortal enemy who's your best friend;
You'd stand alone in a silence that never muttered
Face to face with your emptiness in an empty room.

II

I am so close to you
I will confess to you
I do all you do.
At night I'm flooded by a sense of future
The bursting tide of an unharnessed war,
Drowning the contours of the present.

In thoughts where pity is the same as cruelty
Your life and mine seem one. Whether
What flows and wavers is myself—
Your thoughts in mine or mine in yours—or all
The thoughts crammed in this town—we are the same.

Beyond the windows of a waking dream,
Facts snort their hundred miles an hour
In iron circles on the iron plain.
Speed-bikes and tracks are real: and yet the riders lose
Their sense of place; they're ridden by
Their speed. The men are the machines.

All I can foresee now—more I shall learn—
Is that these fears invent their opposites.
Our peace causes war.
You're coined into a savage when you flee
The crystal civilization dangles.
And when you choose a lover like a mirror
Your own reflection changes to a gunman.
You are a ghost amid wild flares of guns.
Less living than
The shattered dead whose veins of mineral
We mine for now.
                    Alter your life.

III

Dissection of Empires, multiplication of crowns
By secret treaty. Pigeons scatter
Shot off the pavements by the fatal shot.
Heads bounce down stone steps.

Meagre men shoot up. Rockets, rockets,
A corporal's flaming tongue wags above flaming parliament.
The tide of killers now, behold the whip-masters!
Breeches and gaiters camouflage mud.
O visions of a faltering will—
Disintegrating patterns!

History roars. The crowds in towns,
Cerebral frontiers of nations, over mountains,
Actors in flesh and death and matter,
Dance to a gripless orchestra of masses
. . . Thoughts in a dying Chancellor's brain.

Shall I never reach
The field guarded by stones
Rare in the stone mountains
Where the scytheless wind
Flushes the swayed grasses:
Where clouds white without rain
Add to sky and sun
Their lucid sailing shine?
The simple machinery is here
Clear day, clear room, the plain desk,
The hand, symbols of power.
Here the veins may pour
Into the deed, as the field
Into the standing corn.
Meanwhile, where nothing's pious
And truth no longer willed,
Nor the intellect conscious,
Holy is lucidity
And the mind that dare explain.

EXILES FROM THEIR LAND,

HISTORY THEIR DOMICILE

History has tongues
Has angels has guns
           has saved has praised
Her lives-in-exile death-returned
             for whom her printed page
Is heaven on which their wills write worlds.

See how her dead like standards
Planted by Victory in Today
Are capped and cupped by waves!

Planted there, Freedom's fighters—
               One who
Within the stuffed-with-dust-dry darkness
Of a garret, dissected Rome—
               One who
Broke language down to words, then locked each word
Into its hole he docketed—
              Those who met
In a back room with red hot hangings
And planned fury to fall
To set the homes they'd left afire with love—

    (Always outside
    Snow falls, like coatless exiles)

                              One,
A poet, cantered, babbling
Through Twickenham Gardens, where the children
Named him the Dunce's cap to crown all fools.

          Waves now acclaim the truth
Of names that proved their bodies lies,
And books are galleries
Where they become the statues of their wills.

          Death has nothing else to do
But state and stay and make
Them one with what they willed—
                              (Their lives
Were exile from their being)

          [Heroes endure
Horizons ringed with ice, waiting
To break into such tombs where they become
The stars which those who were not, are.]

    •   •   •

          Oh, in those lineaments of immense simplicity
Where is the simularity
With my own wavering uncertainty?
          What divides
Their death my purpose, from my life my weakness?
Their clear dream, from my clear distraction?
Within the eye where is the vision
Within the hands, configuration?

Where, in the momentary flesh,
Is the becomingness of statues
That walk in groves with those who went before?
How am I justified?

        Speak with your tongues,
O angels, fire your guns
                O save and praise
Recall me from this exile
                Let me join
Those who kneel there and kiss the sacred shore

And let my words appear
A heaven-printed world!

AN ELEMENTARY SCHOOL

CLASSROOM IN A SLUM

Far far from gusty waves these children's faces.
Like rootless weeds, the hair torn round their pallor.
The tall girl with her weighed-down head. The paper-
seeming boy, with rat's eyes. The stunted, unlucky heir
Of twisted bones, reciting a father's gnarled disease,
His lesson from his desk. At back of the dim class
One unnoted, sweet and young. His eyes live in a dream
Of squirrel's game, in tree room, other than this.

On sour cream walls, donations. Shakespeare's head,
Cloudless at dawn, civilized dome riding all cities.
Belled, flowery, Tyrolese valley. Open-handed map
Awarding the world its world. And yet, for these
Children, these windows, not this world, are world,
Where all their future's painted with a fog,
A narrow street sealed in with a lead sky,
Far far from rivers, capes, and stars of words.

Surely, Shakespeare is wicked, the map a bad example
With ships and sun and love tempting them to steal—
For lives that slyly turn in their cramped holes
From fog to endless night? On their slag heap, these children
Wear skins peeped through by bones and spectacles of steel
With mended glass, like bottle bits on stones.

All of their time and space are foggy slum.
So blot their maps with slums as big as doom.

Unless, governor, teacher, inspector, visitor,
This map becomes their window and these windows
That shut upon their lives like catacombs,
Break O break open till they break the town
And show the children to green fields, and make their world
Run azure on gold sands, and let their tongues
Run naked into books, the white and green leaves open
History theirs whose language is the sun.

A FOOTNOTE

from Marx's Chapter, The Working Day

'Heard say that four times four is eight,'
'And the King is the Man what has all the Gold.'
'Our King is a Queen and her son's a Princess
'And they live in a Palace called London, I'm told.'

'Heard say that a man called God who's a Dog
'Made the World, with us in it.' 'And then I've heard
'There came a great Flood and the World was all drowned
'Except for one Man, and he was a Bird.'

'So perhaps all the People are dead, and we're Birds
'Shut in steel cages by the Devil, who's good,
'Like the Miners in their pit cages
'And us in our Chimneys to climb, as we should.'

—Ah, twittering voices
Of children crawling on their knees
Through notes of Blue Books, History Books,
At foot of the most crowded pages,
You are the birds of a songless age
Young like the youngest gods, awarded
Mythical childhood always.
Stunted spirits in a fog
Weaving the land

Into tapestries of smoke,
You whisper among wheels,
Calling to your stripped and sacred mothers
With straps tied round their waists
For dragging trucks along a line.
In the sunset above London
Often I watch you lean upon the clouds
Drawn back like a curtain—
O cupids and cherubim
Fixed in the insensate eye
Of a tragic, ignorant age.

When I was young I woke gladly in the morning
With the dew I grieved, towards the close of day.
Now, when I rise, I curse the white cascade
That refreshes all roots, and I wish my eyelids
Were shutters held down by the endless weight
Of the mineral earth. How strange it is, that at evening
When prolonged shadows lie down like cut hay
In my mad age, I rejoice, and my spirit sings
Burning intensely in the centre of a cold sky.

PART THREE

1933-1939

OBSESSIONS

To knock and enter
Knock and enter
The cloudless posthumous door
Where my guts are strung upon a harp that sings of praise
And then to sit and speak
With those who knocked and entered before

In spite of everything
Be justified be justified
At last being at their side who are at my side
To know that this my quality
Of ultimate inferiority
Was on my rounded shoulders the weight of my
          humanity

To look down on my life
That was my life
False social puppet painted with false mouth
Yet in that mouth this voice
That is not quite all death
But its own truth witnessing its justice with living breath

Having accepted then
This weakness beyond dispute

Which is the strength I reject
Blessed weakness reaching back with a dark root
Where earth and womb connect

.   .   .

There is never enough air
There is never wide enough space
There is never blue enough for heaven
There is never white enough for light
There is never a three-dimensional sheet of paper
Where words may climb and dive
And praise loop the loop of aeroplanes

To knock and enter
Knock and enter
The blue ink falling on the white paper
The light falling through the light panes
Of high windows of pure power
The hands resting on the table with controls
Hands with nerves so absolute
They are severed from the wrists
And their thoughts are their fingers

To find release
From the continual headache
And the necessity of such long journeys
Necessity of being alone
And of never being alone
Away from the lighted cities of the brain
To touch and kiss

The dark horizon of the unfulfilled wish
To enter the flower of those who fructify
And fall and fade in the night of desire
To know his flesh-immured secret
Strength whispers to the acrobat

To knock and enter
The ice-bound frigate voyaging to despair
For that also is life that also
Is the journey to the marvellous Rose of snow
To cling to and ride on
The bare-backed quivering human machine
Less swift and soaring than the aeroplane
Rather a clipped domesticated feathered thing
Incapable of flying and yet clinging
To all our lives with all its love

Oh to be taken by it and to hold
My ear against its ever-female heart
To accept its dirt its fleas its little sins
And to explore its mysteries
And nothing to reject or to refuse.

To say I have and I forgive
And that I know this which I hold
Never to slide away among the
Drawing rooms committees hatreds
From what it gives and does not give
This is to walk in that sacred grove

Where voices and ears grow on the same stalk
Bound into sheaves and filled with sun
Of summers that struck and then moved on
And among these to place
This voice my voice posthumous voice

ARCHAIC HEAD

If, without losing this
Confidence of success,
I could go back to those days
And smile through that unhappiness
I wound about us then—
You would see what I now give
Whose intolerable demand
Then, was to touch your hand.
You would see what I have given:
This particular island
Where your archaic head
Is found, having been buried:
Hacked out with words, and read.

To break out of the chaos of my darkness
Into a lucid day, is all my will.
My words like eyes through night, strain to seek
Some centre for their light: and acts that throw me
To distant places through impatient violence
Yet join together to curve a path of stone
Out of my darkness into a lucid day.

Yet, equally, to avoid that lucid day,
And to conserve that darkness, is all my will.
My words like eyes that flinch from light, avoid
The light, and seek their night; my acts
Cast to their opposites by impatient violence
Shatter the sequent path. They move
On a circumference to avoid the centre.

And yet the circumference of my darkness
Throws light on my own weakness at the end;
The iron arc of the avoiding journey
Turns back on me, here where I know I fail;
Whether the faint light spark against my face
Or in the dark my sight hide from my sight,
Centre and circumference are both my weakness.

O strange identity of my will and weakness!
Terrible wave white with the seething word!
Terrible flight through the revolving darkness!
Dreaded light that hunts my profile!
Dreaded night covering me in fears!
My will behind my weakness silhouettes
My territories of fear, with a great sun.

I grow towards the acceptance of that sun
Which hews the day from night. The light
Runs from the dark, the dark from light
Towards a black or white total emptiness.
The world, my life, binds the dark and light
Together, reconciles and separates
In lucid day the chaos of my darkness.

PART FOUR

1936-1939

POEMS ABOUT

THE SPANISH CIVIL WAR

The light in the window seemed perpetual
When you stayed in the high room for me;
It glowed above the trees through leaves
Like my certainty.

The light is fallen and you are hidden
In sunbright peninsulas of the sword:
Torn like leaves through Europe is the peace
That through us flowed.

Now I climb alone to the high room
Above the darkened square
Where among stones and roots, the other
Unshattered lovers are.

THOUGHTS DURING AN

AIR RAID

Of course, the entire effort is to put oneself
Outside the ordinary range
Of what are called statistics. A hundred are killed
In the outer suburbs. Well, well, one carries on.
So long as this thing 'I' is propped up on
The girdered bed which seems so like a hearse,
In the hotel bedroom with the wall-paper
Blowing smoke-wreaths of roses, one can ignore
The pressure of those names under the fingers
Indented by lead type on newsprint,
In the bar, the marginal wailing wireless.
Yet supposing that a bomb should dive
Its nose right through this bed, with one upon it?
The thought's obscene. Still, there are many
For whom one's loss would illustrate
The 'impersonal' use indeed. The essential is
That every 'one' should remain separate
Propped up under roses, and no one suffer
For his neighbour. Then horror is postponed
Piecemeal for each, until it settles on him
That wreath of incommunicable grief
Which is all mystery or nothing.

TWO ARMIES

Deep in the winter plain, two armies
Dig their machinery, to destroy each other.
Men freeze and hunger. No one is given leave
On either side, except the dead, and wounded.
These have their leave; while new battalions wait
On time at last to bring them violent peace.

All have become so nervous and so cold
That each man hates the cause and distant words
That brought him here, more terribly than bullets.
Once a boy hummed a popular marching song,
Once a novice hand flapped their salute;
The voice was choked, the lifted hand fell,
Shot through the wrist by those of his own side.

From their numb harvest, all would flee, except
For discipline drilled once in an iron school
Which holds them at the point of the revolver.
Yet when they sleep, the images of home
Ride wishing horses of escape
Which herd the plain in a mass unspoken poem.

Finally, they cease to hate: for although hate
Bursts from the air and whips the earth with hail

Or shoots it up in fountains to marvel at,
And although hundreds fall, who can connect
The inexhaustible anger of the guns
With the dumb patience of those tormented animals?

Clean silence drops at night, when a little walk
Divides the sleeping armies, each
Huddled in linen woven by remote hands.
When the machines are stilled, a common suffering
Whitens the air with breath and makes both one
As though these enemies slept in each other's arms.

Only the lucid friend to aerial raiders
The brilliant pilot moon, stares down
Upon this plain she makes a shining bone
Cut by the shadows of many thousand bones.
Where amber clouds scatter on No-Man's-Land
She regards death and time throw up
The furious words and minerals which destroy.

The guns spell money's ultimate reason
In letters of lead on the Spring hillside.
But the boy lying dead under the olive trees
Was too young and too silly
To have been notable to their important eye.
He was a better target for a kiss.

When he lived, tall factory hooters never summoned him
Nor did restaurant plate-glass doors revolve to wave him in
His name never appeared in the papers.
The world maintained its traditional wall
Round the dead with their gold sunk deep as a well,
Whilst his life, intangible as a Stock Exchange rumour, drifted
        outside.

O too lightly he threw down his cap
One day when the breeze threw petals from the trees.
The unflowering wall sprouted with guns,
Machine-gun anger quickly scythed the grasses;
Flags and leaves fell from hands and branches;
The tweed cap rotted in the nettles.

Consider his life which was valueless
In terms of employment, hotel ledgers, news files.

Consider. One bullet in ten thousand kills a man.
Ask. Was so much expenditure justified
On the death of one so young, and so silly
Lying under the olive trees, O world, O death?

A STOPWATCH AND AN

ORDNANCE MAP

to Samuel Barber

A stopwatch and an ordnance map.
At five a man fell to the ground
And the watch flew off his wrist
Like a moon struck from the earth
Marking a blank time that stares
On the tides of change beneath.
All under the olive trees.

A stopwatch and an ordnance map.
He stayed faithfully in that place
From his living comrade split
By dividers of the bullet
Opening wide the distances
Of his final loneliness.
All under the olive trees.

A stopwatch and an ordnance map.
And the bones are fixed at five
Under the moon's timelessness;
But another who lives on
Wears within his heart for ever
Space split open by the bullet.
All under the olive trees.

IN NO MAN'S LAND

Only the world changes, and time its tense
Against the creeping inches of whose moons
He launches his rigid continual present.

The grass will grow its summer beard and beams
Of sunlight melt the iron slumber
Where soldiers lie locked in their final dreams.

His corpse be covered with the white December
And roots push through his skin as through a drum
When the years and fields forget, but the bones remember.

THE COWARD

Under the olive trees, from the ground
Grows this flower, which is a wound.
This is wiser to ignore
Than the heroes' sunset fire
Raging with flags on the world's shore.
These blood-dark petals have no name
But the coward's nameless shame.
Here one died, not like a soldier
Of lead, but of rings of terror.
His final moment was the birth
Of naked revelatory truth:
He saw the flagship at the quay,
His mother's care, his lover's kiss,
The white accompaniment of spray,
Lead to the bullet and to this.
Flesh, bone, muscle, eyes,
Built in their noble tower of lies,
Scattered on the icy breeze
Him their false promises betrayed.
All the visions in one instant
Changed to this fixed continual present
Under the grey olive trees.

There's no excuse here for excuse.
Nothing can count but love, to pour
Out its useless comfort here.
To populate his loneliness
And to bring his ghost release
Love and pity dare not cease
For a lifetime, at the least.

FALL OF A CITY

All the posters on the walls,
All the leaflets in the streets
Are mutilated, destroyed, or run in rain,
Their words blotted out with tears,
Skins peeling from their bodies
In the victorious hurricane.

All the names of heroes in the hall
Where the feet thundered and the bronze throats roared
Fox and LORCA claimed as history on the walls,
Are now furiously deleted
Or to dust surrender their gold
From praise excluded.

All the badges and salutes
Torn from lapels and from hands,
Are thrown away with human sacks they wore,
Or in the deepest bed of mind
They are washed over with a smile
Which launches the victors where they win.

All the lessons learned, unlearnt;
The young, who learned to read, now blind
Their eyes with an archaic film;

The peasant relapses to a stumbling tune
Following the donkey's bray;
These only remember to forget.

But somewhere some word presses
In the high door of a skull, and in some corner
Of an irrefrangible eye
Some old man's memory jumps to a child
—Spark from the days of liberty.
And the child hoards it like a bitter toy.

PORT BOU

As a child holds a pet
Arms clutching but with hands that do not join
And the coiled animal looks through the gap
To outer freedom animal air,
So the earth-and-rock arms of this small harbour
Embrace but do not encircle the sea
Which, through a gap, vibrates into the ocean,
Where dolphins swim and liners throb.
In the bright winter sunlight I sit on the parapet
Of a bridge; my circling arms rest on a newspaper
And my mind is empty as the glittering stone
While I search for an image
(The one written above) and the words (written above)
To set down the childish headlands of Port Bou.
A lorry halts beside me with creaking brakes
And I look up at warm downwards-looking faces
Of militiamen staring at my (French) newspaper.
'How do they write of our struggle over the frontier?'
I hold out the paper, but they cannot read it,
They want speech and to offer cigarettes.
In their waving flag-like faces the war finds peace. The
        famished mouths
Of rusted carbines lean against their knees,
Like leaning, rust-coloured, fragile reeds.

Wrapped in cloth—old granny in a shawl—
The stuttering machine-gun rests.
They shout—salute back as the truck jerks forward
Over the vigorous hill, beyond the headland.
An old man passes, his mouth dribbling,
From three rusted teeth, he shoots out: 'pom-pom-pom'.
The children run after; and, more slowly, the women;
Clutching their skirts, trail over the horizon.
Now Port Bou is empty, for the firing practice.
I am left alone on the parapet at the exact centre
Above the river trickling through the gulley, like that old
        man's saliva.
The exact centre, solitary as the bull's eye in a target.
Nothing moves against the background of stage-scenery
        houses
Save the skirring mongrels. The firing now begins
Across the harbour mouth, from headland to headland,
White flecks of foam whipped by lead from the sea.
An echo spreads its cat-o'-nine tails
Thrashing the flanks of neighbour hills.
My circling arms rest on the newspaper,
My mind is paper on which dust and words sift,
I assure myself the shooting is only for practice
But I am the coward of cowards. The machine-gun stitches
My intestines with a needle, back and forth;
The solitary, spasmodic, white puffs from the carbines
Draw fear in white threads back and forth through my body.

TO A SPANISH POET

to Manuel Altolaguirre

You stared out of the window on the emptiness
Of a world exploding;
Stones and rubble thrown upwards in a fountain
Blown to one side by the wind.
Every sensation except being alone
Drained out of your mind.
There was no fixed object for the eye to fix on.
You became a child again
Who sees for the first time how the worst things happen.

Then, stupidly, the stucco pigeon
On the gable roof that was your ceiling,
Parabolized before your window
Uttering (you told me later!) a loud coo.
Alone to your listening self, you told the joke.
Everything in the room broke.
But you remained whole,
Your own image unbroken in your glass soul.

Having heard this all from you, I see you now
—White astonishment haloing irises
Which still retain in their centres
Black laughter of black eyes.

Laughter reverberant through stories
Of an aristocrat lost in the hills near Malaga
Where he had got out of his carriage
And, for a whole week, followed, on foot, a partridge.
Stories of that general, broken-hearted
Because he'd failed to breed a green-eyed bull.

But reading the news, my imagination breeds
The penny-dreadful fear that you are dead.

Well, what of this journalistic dread?

Perhaps it is we—the living—who are dead
We of a world that revolves and dissolves
While we set the steadfast corpse under the earth's lid.
The eyes push irises above the grave
Reaching to the stars, which draw down nearer,
Staring through a rectangle of night like black glass,
Beyond these daylight comedies of falling plaster.

Your heart looks through the breaking ribs—
Oiled axle through revolving spokes.
Unbroken blood of the swift wheel,
You stare through centrifugal bones
Of the revolving and dissolving world.

LOVE AND SEPARATION

TWO KISSES

I wear your kiss like a feather
Laid upon my cheek
While I walk the path where the river
Suggests suggests

Dirt off all the streets
Rotting feet of factories.

Swans and boats and corks ride
Elastic waters
The eye is carried by the choppy tide
To a shore opposite of opal-green spaces
The ear is belied
By dreams inside the roar outside.

Between two sailing swans, a light
Stretches on waves, as on your cheek
That other kiss—my life
Waiting for your life to speak.

THE LITTLE COAT

The little coat embroidered with birds
Is irretrievably ruined.
We bought it in the Spring.
She stood upon a chair
And raised her arms like branches.
I leaned my head against her breast
Listening to that heavy bird
Thudding at the centre of our happiness.

Everything is dragged down and away.
The clothes that were so gay
Lie in attics, like the dolls
With which wild children used to play.
The bed where the loved one lies
Is a river bed on which
Enchanting haunting life
Is borne off where the torrent may—
Nests and singing branches
Tangled among blocks of ice:
Those were the Springs of yesterday.

Hold me in that solemn kiss
Where both our minds have eyes

Which look beyond this
Vanishment: and in each other's gaze
Accept what passes, and believe what stays.

THE VASE OF TEARS

Tears pouring from the face of stone,
Angels from the heart, unhappiness
From some dream to yourself alone—
Let me dry your eyes with these kisses.
I pour what comfort of commonplaces
I can: faint light upon your light alone.
And then we smother with caresses
Both our starved needs to atone.

Cold face creased with human tears. Yet
Something in me tender and delicate
Reads in those eyes an ocean of green water
And one by one these bitter drops collects
Into my heart, a glass vase which reflects
The world's grief weeping in its daughter.

SONG

Stranger, you who hide my love
      In the curved cheek of a smile
And sleep with her upon a tongue
      Of soft lies that beguile,
           Your paradisal ecstasy
      Is justified is justified
By hunger of all beasts beneath
      The overhanging cloud
           Who to snatch quick pleasures run
           Before their momentary sun
Be eclipsed by death.

Lightly, lightly, from my sleep
      She stole, our vows of dew to break
Upon a day of melting rain
      Another love to take;
           Her happy happy perfidy
      Was justified was justified
Since compulsive needs of sense
      Clamour to be satisfied
           And she was never one to miss
           Plausible happiness
Of a new experience.

I, who stand beneath a bitter
          Blasted tree, with the green life
Of summer joy cut from my side
          By that self-justifying knife,
                    In my exiled misery
          Were justified were justified
If upon two lives I preyed
          Or punished with my suicide,
                    Or murdered pity in my heart
                    Or two other lives did part
To make the world pay what I paid.

Oh, but supposing that I climb
          Alone to a high room of clouds
Up a ladder of the time
And lie upon a bed alone
          And tear a feather from a wing
And listen to the world below
And write round my high paper walls
          Anything and everything
Which I know and do not know!

Nipples of bullets, precipices,
Ropes, knives, all
Now would seem as gentle
As the far away kisses
Of her these times remove.

There where thoughts alone
Dance around his walls,
They paint the absent one
Dead and waiting in sweet patience
For him to follow, when she calls.

How can he believe
Her loss is less than his?
'True it may be, she did leave
Me, for another's kiss;
Yet our lives did so entwine
That the blank space of my heart
Torn from hers apart,
Must have torn hers, losing mine.'

Oh, but if he started
On that long journey
Of the fresh-departed,
One and all born poor
Into death naked
Like a slum Bank Holiday
On the grey Lethean shore—

If with nerves strung to a harp
He searched among the spirits there,
Striking the chords to make his wife
Follow him up into life
Out of that leaden place—
He would fail to find there
The folded petals of her face.

For he is no Orpheus,
She no Eurydice.
She has truly packed and gone
To live with someone
Else, in upstairs of the sun.

You must live through the time when everything hurts
When the space of the ripe, loaded afternoon
Expands to a landscape of white heat frozen
And trees are weighed down with hearts of stone
And green stares back where you stare alone,
And the walking eyes throw flinty comments,
And the words which carry most knives are the blind
Phrases searching to be kind.

Solid and usual objects are ghosts
The furniture carries cargoes of memory,
The staircase has corners which remember
As fire blows reddest in gusty embers,
And each empty dress cuts out an image
In fur and evening and summer and spring
Of her who was different in each.

Pull down the blind and lie on the bed
And clasp the hour in the glass of one room
Against your mouth like a crystal doom.
Take up the book and stare at the letters
Hieroglyphs on sand and as meaningless—
Here birds crossed once and a foot once trod
In a mist where sight and sound are blurred.

The story of others who made their mistakes
And of one whose happiness pierced like a star
Eludes and evades between sentences
And the letters break into eyes which read
The story life writes now in your head
As though the characters sought for some clue
To their being transcendently living and dead
In your history, worse than theirs, but true.

Set in the mind of their poet, they compare
Their tragic sublime with your tawdry despair
And they have fingers which accuse
You of the double way of shame.
At first you did not love enough
And afterwards you loved too much
And you lacked the confidence to choose
And you have only yourself to blame.

A girl today, dreaming
On her river of time
With April clouds streaming
Through the glass of her eyes,
Laid down her book,
Looked shoreward, and sighed:

'Oh, if print put on flesh
And these words were whispers
From the lips of the poet
In the vase of my face,
Then this punt would be the river
That bore my name for ever
And my legend never fade.

'Then I would understand
What the people of his land
Never understood: his heart
Was torn apart
By a vulture: hence
Fury his address,
And his life disorder.

'I would cling tight to his hand—
The handle of the glass
Where my image would pass
And I saw my face for ever,'
She thought, turning from her lover
Whose need then hung above her.

And he looked up
Across a gulf of rivers
Straight into a face
High above this time and place
And the terrible eyes knew him
And his terrible eyes knew them.

A SEPARATION

Yes. The will decided. But how can the heart decide,
Lying deep under the surface
Of the level reasons the eye sees—
How can the heart decide
To banish this loved face for ever?

The starry eyes reeded with darkness
To forgo? The light within the body's blindness?
To prove that these were lost in any case
And accept the stumbling stumps of consolation?

Under sleep, under day,
Under the earth, in the tunnel of the marrow,
Unchanging love swears all's unchanged, and knows
That what it has not, still stays all it has.

THE WAR GOD

Why cannot the one good
Benevolent feasible
Final dove, descend?

And the wheat be divided?
And the soldiers sent home?
And the barriers torn down?
And the enemies forgiven?
And there be no retribution?

Because the conqueror
Is victim of his own power
That hammers his heart
From fear of former fear—
When those he now vanquishes
Destroyed his hero-father
And surrounded his cradle
With fabled anguishes.

Today his day of victory
Weeps scalding lead anxiety
Lest children of these slain
Prove dragon teeth (sown

Now their sun goes down)
To rise up one morning
Stain the sky with blood
And avenge their fathers again.

The defeated, filled with lead,
On the helpless field,
May dream the pious reasons
Of mercy, but alas
They know what they did
In their own high seasons.

The world is the world
And not the slain
Nor the slayer, forgive.
There's no heaven above
To make passionate histories
End with endless love.
Yet under wild seas
Of chafing despairs
Love's need does not cease.

AIR RAID ACROSS THE BAY

AT PLYMOUTH

I

Above the whispering sea
And waiting rocks of black coast,
Across the bay, the searchlight beams
Swing and swing back across the sky.

       Their ends fuse in a cone of light
Held for a bright instant up
Until they break away again
Smashing that image like a cup.

II

Delicate aluminum girders
Project phantom aerial masts
Swaying crane and derrick
Above the seas' just lifting deck.

III

Triangles, parallels, parallelograms,
Experiment with hypotheses
On the blackboard sky,
Seeking that X
Where the enemy is met.
Two beams cross
To chalk his cross.

IV

A sound, sounding ragged, unseen
Is chased by Excaliburs of light.
A thud. An instant when the whole night gleams.
Gold sequins shake out of a black-silk screen.

V

Jacob ladders slant
Up to the god of war
Who, from his heaven-high car,
Unloads upon a star
A destroying star.

Round the coast, the waves
Chuckle between rocks.
In the fields the corn
Sways, with metallic clicks.
Man hammers nails in Man,
High on his crucifix.

This early summer prepares its feasts
In the garden, hot on the blossom of the peach,
Fountaining bird song, criss-crossed with bees,
Electric with lizards, packed tight in leaves,
      And the grey First War voices, each to each

Speak, adrift on deck chairs. They say
How little they know of the war not far away,
So different from the mud of France in their day.

Beyond the glaring paths, the blowing
Dust on dog roses in hedges,
Meadows heavy with elms, dusk bringing
Sunday-pressed youths to girls, bicycling
Round War Memorials in villages;

Beyond the tranced summer sea—lines
Cut by keels on its endless glass—
Waves ever moving seeming ever still,
Tiring the day with their permanence of dance,
Beyond the steel Channel like scissors,
Snipping and snipping England from France;

Yes! Beyond those French cliffs, a sound rolls
Ingathering murmurs from inland hills,
Sound of caterpillar-wheeled blond dreams,
Sound of songs cast in steel, mechanically roaring,
Over the larks' nests of France.

'False is the feast this summer—all one garden—
Spreads before our eyes. We must harden.'

'Not the Ear nor the Eye but the Will
Is the organ which alone can make us whole.
Man's world is no more Nature. It is hell
Made by Man-self of which Man must grow well.'

'History is a dragon under human skin.
We must make friends with that evil, if we are to win.'

'Twinned with our lives was our doom
Our killer at our birth, from the same womb.'

'Our indolent injustice, for so long
Snoring over Germany, is overthrown.
To face us with an even greater wrong.'

'So be it, then! The greater wrong must meet
From the less evil, with the worse defeat.'

Afloat on the lawn, the ghostly last war voices
Gaze for a moment through their serge-grey eyes at this:
England chained to the abyss.

Then, wearied unto death, they begin
In disillusioned chorus: 'We shall win!'

But the ghost of one who was young and died,
In the cross-fire of two wars, through the faint leaves sighed:

'I am cold as a cold world alone
Voyaging through space without faith or aim
And no Star whose rays point a Cross to believe in,
And an endless, empty need to atone.'

THE DROWNED

They still vibrate with the sound
Of electric bells,
The sailors who drown
While their mouths and ships fill
With wells of silence
And horizons of distance.

Kate and Mary were cities
Where they lingered on shore
Mingling with the cuties
Who danced on duty there
—With no Sergeant Numb come
To shut down the bar.

No letters reach wrecks
Corpses have no telephone;
Cold tides cut the nerves;
The desires are frozen,
While the blurred sky
Rubs salt medals on the eyes.

Jack sees her with another
And he knows how she smiles
At the light facile rival

Who so simply beguiles
Dancing and doing
What *he* never will now.

Cut off unfairly
By the doom of doom
Which makes heroes and serious
Skulls of us all.
Under waves we now roll
Whose one dream was to play
And forget these bones all day.

The great pulsation passed. Glass lay round me.
Resurrected from dust, I walked
Along streets of slate-jabbering houses,
A prophet seeking tongues of flame.

Against a background of acrid cloud, I saw
The houses kneel, revealed each in its abject
Prayer, my prayer: 'O God, tonight
Spare me from death that punishes my neighbour!'

Then in the sky, indifferent to our
Sulphurous nether hell, I saw
The dead of all pasts float on one calm tide
Among the foam of stars
Above the town, whose walls of brick and flesh
Are transitory dwellings
Of spirits journeying from life to death.

I saw whole streets aflame with London prophets,
Saints of Covent Garden, Parliament Hill Fields,
Hampstead, Hyde Park Corner, Saint John's Wood,
Who cried in cockney fanatic voices:
'In the midst of Life is Death!' They kneeled

And prayed against the misery manufactured
In mines and ships and mills, against
The greed of merchants, vanity of priests.
They played with children and marvelled at the flowers,
And opened their low doors to ask in angels,
Who had once climbed up sooty vents and towers
As steeplejacks and chimney sweeps.

And they sang: 'We souls from the abyss,
Dancing in frozen peace of upper air,
Familiar with the stars in fields of night,
Tell you: 'Rejoice in the abyss!'
For hollow is the skull, the vacuum
In the gold ball under Saint Paul's gold cross.
Unless you will accept the emptiness
Within the bells of fox-gloves and cathedrals,
Each life must feed upon the deaths of others
And the shamelessly entreating prayer
Of every head will be that it is spared
Calamity that strikes his neighbour.'

A MAN-MADE WORLD

What a wild room
We enter, when the gloom
Of windowless night
Shuts us from the light

In man's black malicious box.
Then a key locks
Us into the utter dark
Where the nerves hark

For the man-made toys
To whirr with wound-up noise.
The siren wails. After,
Broomsticks climb air,

Clocks break through springs,
Then the fire bell rings.
From high and low comes,
Rage of the drums.

Ah, what white rays gleaming
Up to the sky's low ceiling!
Ah, what flashes show
A woman who cries: 'Oh!'

Thus the world we made
Pays back what we paid;
Thus the dark descends
On our means become our ends.

MEMENTO

Remember the blackness of that flesh
Tarring the bones with a thin varnish
Belsen Theresenstadt Buchenwald where
Faces were a clenched despair
Knocking at the bird-song-fretted air.

Their eyes sunk jellied in their holes
Were held up to the sun like begging bowls
Their hands like rakes with finger-nails of rust
Scratched for a little kindness from the dust.
To many, in its beak, no dove brought answer.

THE FATES

I

Which are the actors, which the audience?
Those who sit back and listen and don't say
Or those on the stage who open ribs like doors,
To show their hearts, lift up their skulls like lids
Reveal their wit like a Jack-in-the-box,
Are salted with the savour of corruption
And scented with the opera-singing organs?
Who hold hidden in language, like an attic in a castle,
A high bare room large as infinite space,
Where the soul plays at being a gull by a lake,
Turns somersaults, is eternally bored,
Whistles to itself, keeps a journal read by God,
Remembering and forgetting
What the undertakers undertake?

Oh which are the actors, which the audience?
The players, who simulate?
Or those who are, who watch the actors
Prove the unreal, that fate is no fate?
Which are the actors, which the audience?
Which is the real performance
Finally sweeping actors and audience
Into a black box on the dead-line date?

You wore that painted mask of motherhood
For twenty years, while you denied the real
Was anything but the exceptional.
You were the family stage manager
For your son's sake, and your great house his theatre
Where all the plays were musicals, or light;
'This is the stage where nothing happens that can matter
Except that we look well produced and bright.'

Your problem was no easy one:
Somehow to spare your only son
From the burden cloud grey in his father's eyes,
Between two wars, for twenty years
Pacing the lawn, between two wars,
His too-fixed way of glooming at the table.
You were courageous and capable.
Rightly, you called these moods his 'moods'.
Moods, moods, moods, like fires or hells,
Chairs, pictures and the passing of alarm bells.

You rebuilt the Georgian house, returfed the lawn,
Planted the kitchen garden in its wall
And the servants in the servants' hall.
They tidied the downstairs rooms at dawn;
And you bought a fishing rod, a pony and a gun
And gave these to your son.

The fresh air and the scenery did the rest.
He ripened, and his laughter floated on the lake,
A foretaste of those memories that suggest
His photograph with the shirt open at the neck.
He ran downstairs to dinner, 'dressed'.
Then your happiness bound cords
Around his treasured glance, like a blue bow.
Catching your husband's eyes, your eyes spoke words
'This is the world. We've left the fates below.'

If there were a guest, who in the course
Of gossip, spoke of 'so-and-so's divorce,'
Or else 'Poor Lady X, she died of cancer,'
You had your fine frank answer,
Questioning him with vivid curiosity:
Poverty, adultery, disease, what next monstrosity!
You smiled, perhaps at your guest's eccentricity,
Who'd laid such specimens out on the floor.

Your son grew up, and thought it all quite real.
Hunting, the family, the business man's ideal.
The poor, and the unhappy, had his sympathy.
They were exceptions, born to prove his rule.
And yet he had his moments of uneasiness
When, in the dazzling garden of his family,
With green sunlight reflected on your dress,
His body suddenly seemed an obscenity,
A changeling smuggled to the wrong address.

Still, he got married. *She,* was dull of course.
But everything had turned out quite all right.
The bride sailed on the picture page in white.
She looked a little hard, in the hard light.
He wore uniform. You, now mother-in-law,
Who'd brought him up into a world at war,
Suddenly, you felt tired. What does he know of life?
—You thought. Enough to satisfy his wife,
He'd learned from you, and shooting, and his horse.

III

Oh, but in vain
Do men bar themselves behind their doors
Within the seemly and appointed house
Delineating life in manners,
The fire in the grate, the flowers in the vase, the laden table.

The storm rises
The thunderbolt falls, and how feeble
Is the long ritual
Though up-to-date its shell
Strengthened with steel and concrete.

The walls fall, tearing down
The mother-of-pearl inlaid interior.
The cultivated fire leaps from the grate
Consumes the house, the cat reverts to tiger
Leaping out of a world changed back to jungle
To claw her master.

The parents fall
Clutching at the beams that snap like straw.
The handsome only son
Tanned leader of his village team
Is shaken out of the silk folds
Of sprinkled lawns, as from a curtain.

He is thrown out on to a field abroad.
A whip of lead
Strikes a stain of blood from his pure forehead.
Into the dust he falls,
Oval face carved from a mother's kisses
Eternally chaste ivory
Fallen back, staring at the sun, the eyes at last cut open.

When pavements were blown up, exposing nerves,
And the gas mains burned blue and gold,
And stucco and brick were pulverized to a cloud
Pungent with smells of mice, dust, garlic, anxiety:
When the reverberant emptied façades
Of the West End palaces of commerce
Isolated in a vacuum of silence, suddenly
Cracked and blazed and fell, with the seven-maned
Lions of Wrath licking the stony fragments—

Then the one voice through deserted streets
Was the Cassandra bell which rang and rang and ran
Released at last by Time
To seek those fires that burst through many walls—
Prophetic doom laid bare under the nostrils,
Blood and fire streaming from the stones.

London burned with unsentimental dignity
Of resigned kingship: those stores and Churches
Which had glittered century-long in dusty gold
Stood near the throne of domed St. Paul's
Like courtiers round the Royal sainted martyr.
August shadows of night

And bursting shells of concentrated light
Dropped from the skies to paint a final scene
Illuminated agony of frowning stone.
Who then can wonder that every word
In burning London, stepped out of a play?

On the stage, there were heroes, maidens, fools,
Victims, a Chorus. The heroes were brave,
The fools spat jokes into the skull of death,
The victims waited with the humble patience
Of animals trapped behind a wall
For the pickaxes to break, with light and water.
The Chorus assisted, bringing cups of tea,
Praising the heroes, deploring the morals of the wicked,
Underlining punishment, justifying Doom to Truth.

PART SEVEN

1944

EXPLORATIONS

To Cecil Day Lewis

We fly through a night of stars
Whose remote frozen tongues speak
A language of mirrors, Greek to Greek,
Flashing across space, each to each.
O night of Venus and Mars,
In a dance of life extinct, far far far from these wars.

I

Within our nakedness, nakedness still
Is the naked mind. Past and stars show
Through the columned bones. Tomorrow
Will blow away the temple of each will.
The Universe, by inches, minutes, fills
Our hollowed tongues. Name and image glow
In word, in form. Star and history know
That they exist, in life existence kills.
        Revolving on the earth rim through the night,
Homunculi, pulsing blood and breath,
Separate in separation, yet unite
For that last journey to no place nor date,
Where, naked beneath nakedness, beneath
Each, all are nothing, who await
The multitudinous loneliness of death.

II

Were born; must die; were loved; must love;
Born naked; were clothed, still naked, walk
Under your dress. Under your skin, move
Naked, naked under acts and talk.
Miles and hours upon you feed.
They eat your eyes out with their avid distance
They eat your heart out with their empty need;
They eat your soul out with vanished significance.
One fate is sure beneath those ignorances
Of flesh and bone packet in which you're split,
Patchwork deed and word hanging on breath:
Mandolin skeleton, it
Strums on your gut such songs and peasant dances,
Solitudo, amor, O life, O death.

III

Since we are what we are, what shall we be
But what we are? We are, we have
Six feet and seventy years, to see
The light, and then resign it for the grave.
We are not worlds, no, nor infinity,
We have no claims on stone, except to prove
In the invention of the human city
Ourselves, our breath, our death, our love.
          The tower we build soars like an arrow
From the earth's rim towards the sky's,
Upwards-downwards in a star-filled pond,

Climbing and diving from our world, to narrow
The gap between the world shut in the eyes
And the receding world of light beyond.

IV

Exiles from single Being of Belief,
They know inextricable knots which bind
Each to himself; blind walls that blind
Their eyes revolving inwardly in grief.
Each circular self saws round his little leaf
Whose closed serrated edge is his own kind.
Dreams of a vast Outside inside each mind
May tempt with world each one to be a thief.
        And yet they are not aeons, they are not space,
Not empires, not maps: they are only
Heads dreaming pictures, each fixed in his place.
And Geography and History are unfurled
Within each separate skull, grown lonely
With Time, making, shedding, a World.

V

The Immortal Spirit is that single ghost
Of every time incarnate in one time
Which to achieve its timelessness must climb
Our bodies, and in our senses be engrossed.
Without that Spirit within, our lives are lost
Fragments, disturbing the earth's rim.
Unless we will it live, that God pines, dim,
Ghost in our lives: its life, our death, the cost.

The Spirit of present, past, futurity
Seeks through the many-headed wills
To build the invisible visible city.
Shut in himself, each blind, beaked subject kills
His neighbour and himself, and shuts out pity
For that flame-winged Creator who fulfils.

VI

One is the witness through whom the whole
Knows it exists. Within his coils of blood,
Drumming under his sleep, there moves the flood
Of stars, battles, dark and glacial pole.
One is all that one is not. On his dreams ride
Dead ancestors. All spaces outside
Glitter under his ribs. Being all things, one is one.
I who say I call that eye I
Which is the mirror in which things see
Nothing except themselves. I die.
The world, the things seen, still will be.
Upon this eye the vast reflections lie
But that which passes, passes away, is I.

PART EIGHT

ELEGY FOR MARGARET

These poems are inscribed to the memory of
Margaret Spender, who died on Christmas Day, 1945

ELEGY FOR MARGARET

I

Darling of our hearts, drowning
In the thick night of ultimate sea
Which (indeed) surrounds us all, but where we
Are crammed islands of flesh, wide
With a few harvesting years, disowning
The bitter black severing tide;

Here in this room you are outside this room,
Here in this body your eyes drift away,
While the invisible vultures feed on
Your life, and those who read the doom
Of the ill-boding omens say
Name of a disease, which, like a villain

Seizes on the pastures of your flesh,
Then gives you back some acres, soon again
To set you on that rack of pain
Where the skeleton cuts through you like a knife,
And the weak eyes flinch with their hoping light
Which, where we wait, blinds our still hoping sight.

Until hope signs us to despair—what lives
Seems what most kills—what holds back fate

Seems itself fated—and the eyes that smile
Mirror the mocking illness that contrives
Moving away some miles
To ricochet at one appointed date.

Least of our world, yet you are most this world
Today, when those who are well are those who hide
In dreams painted by unfulfilled desire
From hatred triumphing outside:
And where the brave, who live and love, are hurled
Through waters of a flood shot through with fire;

Where sailors' eyes rolling on floors of seas
Hold in their luminous darkening irises
The memory of some lost still dancing girl,
The possible attainable happy peace
Of statued Europe with its pastures fertile,
Dying, like a girl, of a doomed, hidden disease.

So, to be honest, I must wear your death
Next to my heart, where others wear their love.
Indeed it is my love, my link with life
My word of life being knowledge of such death.
My dying word because of you can live,
Crowned with your death, this life upon my breath.

II

From a tree choked by ivy, rotted
By kidney-shaped fungus on the bark,

Out of a topmost branch,
A spray of leaves is seen
That shoots against the ice-cold sky its mark.
The dying tree still has the strength to launch
The drained life of the sap
Into that upward arrowing glance
Above the strangling cords of evergreen.

So with you, Margaret,
Where you are lying,
The tree-trunk of your limbs choked back
By what destroys you—yet
Above the sad grey flesh
What smile surmounts your dying
On the peak of your gaze!

How tediously time kills
While the difficult breath
Asserts one usual, laughing word
Above this languor of death.
Like a water-clock it fills
The hollow well of bones
Drop by drop with dying—
Yet all that life we knew,
The eyes hold still.

How, when you have died,
Shall we remember to forget,
And with knives to separate
This life from this death:

Since, Margaret, there is never a night,
But the beflagged pride of your youth
In all its joy, does not float
Upon my sleep, as on a boat.

III

Poor girl, inhabitant of a stark land,
Where death covers your gaze,
As though the full moon might
Cast over the midsummer blaze
Its bright and dead white pall of night.

Poor child, you wear your summer dress,
And black shoes striped with gold
As today its variegated cover
Of feathery grass and spangling flowers
Delineating colour over
Shadows within which bells are tolled.

I look into your sunk eyes,
Shafts of wells to both our hearts
Which cannot take part in the lies
Of acting these gay parts.
Under our lips, our minds
Become one with the weeping
Of that mortality
Which through sleep is unsleeping.

Of what use is my weeping?
It does not carry a surgeon's knife

To cut the wrongly-multiplying cells
At the root of your life.
All it can prove
Is that extremes of love
Reach the Arctic Pole of the white bone
Where panic fills our night all night alone.

Yet my grief for you is myself, a dream,
Tomorrow's light will sweep away.
It does not wake day after day
To the same facts that are and do not seem:
The changeless changing facts around your bed,
Poverty-stricken hopeless ugliness
Of the fact that you will soon be dead.

IV

i

Already you are beginning to become
Fallen tree-trunk with sun-sculptured limbs
In a perspective of dead branches and dry bones
Encircled by encroaching monumental stones.

ii

Those that begin to cease to be your eyes
Are flowers whose petals fade and honey dries
Crowded over with end-of-summer butterflies.
Wings gather to night's thickening memories.
Peacock, Red Admiral, Fritillaries,
Fly to your eyes and then fly from our gaze.

iii

Against the wall, you are already partly ghost
Whispering scratching existence almost lost
To our vulgar blatant life that eats through rooms
Our vulgar blatant life like heaped-up transient blooms.

iv

You are so quiet; your hand on the sheet seems a mouse
Yet when we turn away, the flails
That pound and beat you down with ceaseless pulse
Shake like steam hammers through the house.

v

Evening brings the opening of the windows.
Now your last sunset throws
Shadows from the roots of trees
Thrusting hounds it unleashes.
In the sky fades the cinder of a rose.
The Eumenides strain forwards.
The pack of night stretches towards us.

v

The final act of love
Is not of dear and dear
Blue-bird-shell eye pink-sea-shell ear
Dove twining neck with dove;

Oh no, it is the world-storm fruit
Sperm of tangling distress,

Mouth raging in the wilderness,
Fingernail tearing at dry root.

The deprived, fanatic lover
Naked in the desert
Of all except his heart
In his abandon must cover

With wild lips and torn hands,
With blanket made from his own hair,
With comfort made from his despair
The sexless corpse laid in the sands.

He pursues that narrow path
Where the cheek leads to the skull
And the skull into spaces, full
Of lilies, and death.

Dazed, he finds himself among
Saints, who slept with hideous sins,
Whose tongues take root on ruins,
And their language fills his tongue:

'How far we travelled, sweetheart,
Since that day when first we chose
Each other as each other's rose
And put all other men apart.

'Now we assume this coarseness
Of loved and loving bone

Where all are all and all alone
And to love means to bless
Everything and everyone.'

VI

to J.H.S.

Dearest and nearest brother,
No words can turn to day
The freezing night of silence
Where all your dawns delay
Watching flesh of your Margaret
Wither in sickness away.

Yet those we lose, we learn
With singleness to love:
Regret stronger than passion holds
Her the times remove:
All those past doubts of life, her death
One happiness does prove.

Better in death to know
The happiness we lose
Than die in life in meaningless
Misery of those
Who lie beside chosen
Companions they never chose.

Orpheus, maker of music,
Clasped his pale bride
Upon that terrible river

Of those who have died;
Then of his poems the uttermost
Laurel sprang from his side.

When your red eyes follow
Her body dazed and hurt
Under the torrid mirage
Of delirious desert,
Her breasts break with white lilies,
Her eyes with Margaret.

I bring no consolation
Of the weeping shower
Whose final dropping jewel deletes
All grief in the sun's power:
You must watch the signs grow worse
Day after day, hour after hour.

Yet to accept the worst
Is finally to revive
When we are equal with the force
Of that with which we strive
And having almost lost, at last
Are glad to be alive.

As she will live who, candle-lit
Floats upon her final breath
The ceiling of the frosty night
And her high room beneath,
Wearing not like destruction, but
Like a white dress, her death.

PART NINE

1941–1949

MEETINGS AND ABSENCE

THE DREAM

'You dream,' he said, 'because of the child
Asleep in the nest of your body, who dreams. . . .'

Her lips dreamt, and he smiled.

He laid his head, weighed with a thought
On the sleep of her lips. Thus locked
Within the lens of their embrace
They watched the life their lives had wrought,

Watched within her flesh complete
The future folded active street
Straddling with gold cock-crowing face,
Between their cradle bodies rocked.

ONE

Here then
She lies
Her hair a scroll along
The grooved warm nape
Her lips half-meeting on a smile
Breath almost unbreathing
O life
A word this word my love upon the white
Linen
As though I wrote her name out on this page.

My concentra-
tion on her quietness
Intensifies like light ringed from this lamp
That throws its halo upward on the ceiling

Here we
Are one
Here where my waking walks upon her sleep
One within one
And darkly meeting in the hidden child.

ABSENCE

No one is perfection, yet
When, being without you, I console
Myself, by dwelling on some blemish
Once marked, which now might seem to mar the whole,
Telling myself your absence might become my wish,

Oh then, that barrier which I set
Between us, vanishes.
I see only the pure you of your eyes.
Distances between us lying
Open like a gate
Through which our mutual memories meet
Uniting wishes.

DAYBREAK

At dawn she lay with her profile at that angle
Which, when she sleeps, seems the carved face of an angel.
Her hair a harp, the hand of a breeze follows
And plays, against the white cloud of the pillows.
Then, in a flush of rose, she woke, and her eyes that opened
Swam in blue through her rose flesh that dawned.
From her dew of lips, the drop of one word
Fell like the first of fountains: murmured
'Darling,' upon my ears the song of the first bird.
'My dream becomes my dream,' she said, 'come true.
I waken from you to my dream of you.'
Oh, my own wakened dream then dared assume
The audacity of her sleep. Our dreams
Poured into each other's arms, like streams.

LOST

Horizontal on amber air, three boughs of green
Lift slotted sleeves. Beyond them, the house glows.
Straight mouldings delineate tall windows.
Glass panes hold the balance between
Garden mirrored and interior darkly seen.

That cracked stucco wall seems the harsh rind
Of a fruit, guarding sweetness I savour:
My dreams, like teeth, penetrate the flavour
Of its honeyed withheld life behind
Whose taste once entered me, body and mind.

Against that wall my hungry memories press
To reach back to the time that was my heart.
One room, my heart, holds a girl with lips apart
Watching a child, starry in nakedness,
Her gaze covers him like a fleecy dress.

This is that room where the world was most precious.
Jewelled silence in their eyes collects
Light, that each from each all day reflects.
Here life and furniture are gracious,
All times and places outside here, atrocious.

My spirit, strayed in wars abroad, seems ghost
Gazing through gales and clay on his warm past.
Now from my empty everywhere I cast
Unseen unseeing glances through time lost
Back to that sole room where life was life most.

SEASCAPE

In Memoriam, M.A.S.

There are some days the happy ocean lies
Like an unfingered harp, below the land.
Afternoon gilds all the silent wires
Into a burning music for the eyes.
On mirrors flashing between fine-strung fires
The shore, heaped up with roses, horses, spires,
Wanders on water, walking above ribbed sand.

The motionlessness of the hot sky tires
And a sigh, like a woman's, from inland
Brushes the instrument with shadowing hand
Drawing across its wires some gull's sharp cries
Or bell, or shout, from distant, hedged-in shires;
These, deep as anchors, the hushing wave buries.

Then from the shore, two zig-zag butterflies,
Like errant dog-roses, cross the bright strand
Spiralling over sea in foolish gyres
Until they fall into reflected skies.
They drown. Fishermen understand
Such wings sunk in such ritual sacrifice,

Recalling legends of undersea, drowned cities.
What voyagers, oh what heroes, flamed like pyres

With helmets plumed, have set forth from some island
And them the sea engulfed. Their eyes,
Contorted by the cruel waves' desires
Glitter with coins through the tide scarcely scanned,
While, above them, that harp assumes their sighs.

THE BARN

Half hidden by trees, the sheer roof of the barn
Is a river of tiles, warped
By winding currents of weather
Suns and storms ago.

Through beech leaves, its vermilion seems
A Red Admiral's wing, with veins
Of lichen and rust, an underwing
Of winter-left leaves.

Now, in the Spring, a sapling's jet
Of new, pure flame, cuts across
The low long gutter. One leaf holds up
Red tiles reflected in its cup.

At the side of the road where cars crash past,
The barn lies under the sky like a throat
Full of dark gurgitation:

A ghost of a noise—a hint of a gust
Caught in the rafters centuries ago:
The creak of a winch, the wood turn of a wheel.

Entangled in murmurs, as in a girl's hair,
Is the enthusiastic scent
Of course, yellow straw—lit by that sunbeam,
Which, laden with motes, strikes across the floor.

DUSK

Steel edge of plough
Thrusts through the stiff
Ruffled field of turfy
Cloud in the sky.
Above charcoal hedges
And dead leaf land
It cuts out a deep
Gleaming furrow
Of glass, where we look
From our darkening day
Up a funnel, at stars.

On earth below,
Men's knotted hands
Lay down tired tasks.
Wooden handles
Of spade implements
Rest on the ground.
Shuffling animals
Wrinkling muzzles
Sniff the sweet passing peace,
And twitching their ears
Hear bells on the breeze.

The set will of man
Floats loose, released.
Dusk drops a dark cloak
So wide it encloses
The entire universe.
Terracotta
Deletes all detail,
Robs one by one
Stones from villages
Petals from flowers,
Words from men.

Names fall away,
With a spasm, nakedness
Assumes mankind.
Man's mind, cast adrift,
On his bed upstairs,
Awaits the anchorage
Of sleep, while he dreams
Worst dreams—those that wake.

A great lost river
Crepitates
Through dry creaks of his brain.
Long-buried days
Rise out of tombs
With fists that unfold
Lost powers they held.

Now the burning eye
Of One outside time,
Stares through the limbs
Of brief manalive
Dredging up memories
Of reptiles and apes,
Bronze and stone trophies.

What fearful dreams
Mock his brief day
Filled with brief aims—
Robbing his neighbour
Killing his neighbour.
O turn back from that sleep
Shut your eyes to that terror
Of love, and wake
To daybreak's heartbreak—
Habitual hatred.

MEETING

Que mon amour a la semblance
Du beau Phénix, s'il meurt un soir
Le Matin voit sa Renaissance.

APOLLINAIRE

I

At dawn we rose and walked the pavement

I your shadow you my flute

Your voice wove a thread
Through Paris in my head

I followed followed
You my sole inhabitant.

II

'At last,' you sang, 'there comes this peace
Beyond War's separating will,
Where we are alone, face to face.

'If tomorrow divide us, we shall fill
That space with this peace as today the space
Which, when we are closest, must divide us still.

'Distances between us are of crystal
Traversed with diagonals of rays
In which our eyes meet when, near or far, they gaze.

'Gazing into that crystal, behold the possible
Nakedness nakeder than nakedness
Where, stripped of Time and Place, as of a dress,
We shall meet again, although invisible,

'Farewell now——'

III

                    Just then the sun scrawled
Across the blank sheet of the day
Twisted iron realities
Broken boulevards where humanity's
Sprawling River Styx
Of victims through their own war shadows crawled.

Oh but we were the Phoenix——

IV

We were the two sides of one vase
Gaze flowed into gaze
Under the surfaces
Of our curved embraces

Our eyes see with each other's eyes
Half a world between us lies
Your night holds my light
My day's mystery is your night

These words are both our silences
One glass holds both our distances

On my tongue your tongue
Rustles with your song my song

V

Into my heart there sang the words
The lips no sooner uttered
Than they seemed in their concords
Not mine I said but yours I heard.

The distances that separate
Have driven our lives through that gate
Beyond which our impossible
Meeting becomes invisible,
Meeting indivisible.

I C E

to M——

She came in from the snowing air
Where icicle-hung architecture
Strung white fleece round the Baroque square.
I saw her face freeze in her fur,
Then my lips ran to her with fire
From the chimney corner of the room,
Where I had waited in my chair.
I kissed their heat against her skin
And watched the red make the white bloom,
While, at my care, her smiling eyes
Shone with the brilliance of the ice
Outside, whose dazzling they brought in.
      That day, until this, I forgot.
How is it now I so remember
Who, when she came indoors, saw not
The passion of her white December?

WORD

The word bites like a fish.
Shall I throw it back free
Arrowing to that sea
Where thoughts lash tail and fin?
Or shall I pull it in
To rhyme upon a dish?

THE TRANCE

Sometimes, apart in sleep, by chance,
You fall out of my arms, alone,
Into the chaos of your separate trance.
My eyes gaze through your forehead, through the bone,
And see where in your sleep distress has torn
Its violent path, which on your lips is shown
And on your hands and in your dream forlorn.

Restless, you turn to me, and press
Those timid words against my ear
Which thunder at my heart like stones.
'Mercy,' you plead, Then 'Who can bless?'
You ask. 'I am pursued by Time,' you moan.
I watch that precipice of fear
You tread, naked in naked distress.

To that deep care we are committed
Beneath the wildness of our flesh
And shuddering horror of our dream,
Where unmasked agony is permitted.
Our bodies, stripped of clothes that seem,
And our souls, stripped of beauty's mesh,
Meet their true selves, their charms outwitted.

This pure trance is the oracle
That speaks no language but the heart,
Our angel with our devil meets
In the atrocious dark nor do they part
But each each forgives and greets,
And their mutual terrors heal
Within our married miracle.

O

O thou O
Of round earth of round heaven,
Unfold thy wings,
Then beyond the colour blue
Pass, beyond light
Pass, into space, out of sight

Beyond sight
O, into pure sound
Where one trumpet
Sustains the final note,
O pass beyond sound
Into pure silence

Beyond silence
O at the throne of God
Beyond flesh pass
Beyond form to idea
O metamorphosis
Beyond God to godlessness.

Return now
To thyself, O,

Bite thy own tail
Hoop thy own hoop

Loop thy own loop
Become that hole
Through which the eye leaps
Beyond the page, O
Word of beginning with
Omega end.

IN ATTICA

Again, again, I see this form repeated:
The bare shadow of a rock outlined
Against the sky; declining gently to
An elbow; then the scooped descent
From the elbow to the wrist of a hand that rests
On the plain.
                    Again, again,
That arm outstretched from the high shoulder
And leaning on the land.
                                        As though the torsoed
Gods, with heads and lower limbs broken off,
Plunged in the sky, or buried under earth,
Had yet left arms extended here as pointers
Between the sun and plain:
                                        had made this landscape
Human, like Greek steles, where the dying
Are changed to stone on a gesture of curved air,
Lingering in their infinite departure.

MESSENGER

to Georges Seferis

O messenger, held back
From your journey!—walled in,
Imagination trails leaves
Shut from the sun!

•   •   •

In what cellar of his brain
A map flashes with
The island-sprinkled sea, and
Mountain-vertebrate land
—Osseous hand
Whose fingers spread
Peninsulas. His eyes
Cut the day
Out of sunlight all day,
Diamonds of the light
Shed on agate hills
Their gleams all night.

Upon one headland
Marble foot treads.
Sunium. Columns at edge
Of keel-scarred Aegean.

His hot will races
Through brake and flint.
Anemone, rock rose,
Asphodel, thyme,
Tear his thighs.
To the temple he runs
And kisses the white stone.

Before he can
Say what he can,
He lifts his eyes where
Grooved columns are quivers
From which the archer sun
Takes arrows to shoot
Through his eye-sockets.

Above the temple rooflessness,
Clouds are a roof
Remembering lines
Of a frieze whose procession
Fell out of the sky.
On a wave of the air
Hands, simple as light,
Bent. Their tunics
Were marble breeze.
Embossed hooves
Of quadruple quadrupeds
Oxen and horses,
Stamped. Manes were crests

Of torches which burned
Through nostrils hewn like eyes.

A clear chisel cut
These lines taut as knots
Which yet have the freedom
To un-knot hearts.
The raised hand of a god
Has blood through veins where
The human flows into
The absolute.

What message speaks
From the new ruined Europe
To the old, ruined Greece?
None! Yet believe in
Words where worlds cross
Where all that is not
Must swear: 'I am!'

EMPTY HOUSE

to M.F.M.S.

Then, when the child was gone,
I was alone
In the house, suddenly grown vast. Each noise
Explained its origin away
—Animal, vegetable, mineral,
Nail, creaking board, or little mouse.
But mostly there was quiet of after battle
Round the room where lay
The soldiers and the paint-box, all the toys.
        Then, when I went to tidy these away,
My hands refused to serve:
My body was this house,
Each plaything that he'd touched, an exposed nerve.

TO MY DAUGHTER

Bright clasp of her whole hand around my finger,
My daughter, as we walk together now.
All my life I'll feel a ring invisibly
Circle this bone with shining: when she is grown
Far from today as her eyes are far already.

MISSING MY DAUGHTER

This wall-paper has lines that rise
Upright like bars, and overhead,
The ceiling's patterned with red roses.
On the wall opposite the bed
The staring looking-glass encloses
Six roses in its white of eyes.

Here at my desk, with note-book open
Missing my daughter, makes those bars
Draw their lines upward through my mind.
This blank page stares at me like glass
Where stared-at roses wish to pass
Through petalling of my pen.

An hour ago, there came an image
Of a beast that pressed its muzzle
Between bars. Next, through tick and tock
Of the reiterating clock
A second glared with the wide dazzle
Of deserts. The door, in a green mirage,

Opened. In my daughter came.
Her eyes were wide as those she has,

The round gaze of her childhood was
White as the distance in the glass
Or on a white page, a white poem.
The roses raced around her name.

NOCTURNE

Their six-weeks-old daughter lies
In her cot, crying out the night. Their hearts
Are sprung like armies, waiting
To cross the gap to where her loneliness
Lies infinite between them. This child's cry
Sends rays of a star's pain through endless dark;
And the sole purpose of their loving
Is to disprove her demonstration
Of all love's aidlessness. Words unspoken
Out of her mouth unsaying, prove unhappiness
Pure as innocence, virgin of tragedy,
Unknowing reason. Star on star of pain
Surround her cry to make a constellation
Where human tears of victims are the same
As griefs of the unconscious animals.

        Listening, the parents know this primal cry
Out of the gates of life, hollows an emptiness
That proves men's aims should be, all times,
To fill the gap of pain with consolation
Poured from the mountain-sided adult lives
Whose minds like peaks attain to heights of snow:
The snow should stoop to wash away such grief.
Unceasing love should lave the feet of victims.

Yet, when they lift their heads out of such truths,
Today mocks at their prayers. To think this even
Suffices to remind them of far worse
Man-made man-destroying ills which threaten
While they try to lull a child. For she
Who cries for milk, for rocking, and a shawl,
Is also subject to the rage of causes
Dividing peoples. Even at this moment
Eyes might fly between them and the moon,
And a hand touch a lever to let fall
That which would make the street of begging roofs
Pulverize and creep skywards in a tower:
Down would fall baby, cradle, and them all.

That which sent out the pilot to destroy them
Was the same will as that with which they send
An enemy to kill their enemy. Even in this love
Running in shoals on each side of her bed,
Is fear, and hate. If they shift their glances
From her who weeps, their eyes meet other eyes
Willed with death, also theirs. All would destroy
New-born, innocent streets. Necessity,
With abstract head and searing feet, men's god
Unseeing the poor amulets of flesh,
Unhearing the minutiae of prayer.

Parents like mountains watching above their child,
Envallied here beneath them, also hold
Upon their frozen heights, the will that sends
Destruction into centres of the stones

Which concentrated locked centennial stillness
For human generations to indwell.

      Hearing their daughter's cry which is the speech
Of indistinguishable primal life,
They know the dark is filled with means which are
Men's plots to murder children. They know too
No cause is just unless it guards the innocent
As sacred trust: no truth but that
Which reckons this child's tears an argument.

Places I shared with her, things that she touched—
Could I ever have known
How untouchable these would become
The day after she was gone?

Sirmio's peninsula stretches out into the lake
Like one spoke thrusting to the centre
Of the mountain-circled water: where
I stand now, through brush-branched olive trees
And ragged broken arches
Ancient Romans built so long ago,
I see the water's bowl-edge round me, in an almost perfect O.

This I saw once before, with her, as long it seems now,
As though I were one of those Romans. I noticed then
The wings of the water flashing through torn-brick arches
The olive leaves turned by the sky from silver to blue,
The lizards shocks through the grass,
The mountains ringed glassily round the lake, seeming
Gray dolphins painted on glass.

I watched and watched then as I watch and watch now. And
        she who was with me seemed sad
Seeing me self-enclosed in my view of the view

That shut her out from me, as though at my desk in my room,
In the midst of our Lake Garda honeymoon.
Now the mountains might fall and crush me. All the wide rim
Of their up-diving shapes from the water, brings pain
Of unapproachable things
Making me conscious that I am unseeing alone
Since she with whom I would be is not at my side,
With her hair blown back by the winds of the whole lake
          view,
Lips parted as though to greet the flight of a bird.

DYLAN THOMAS

November 1953

In November of Catherine Wheels and rockets
This roaring ranter, man and boy,
Proved Guy Fawkes true, and burned on a real fire.
His rhymes that stuffed his body were the straw,
His poems he shed out of his pockets,
Were squibs and sweets and string and wire,
The crackling gorse thorn crowned him with spiked joy.

Where he sang, burning, round his neck a cup
Begged: 'Pennies, pennies, for the Guy!'
And every coin from every passer by
When it was melted, he drank fiery up.
And all his sins, before his voice that spoke,
Shot angels skywards. Now, that he should die
Proves the fire was the centre of his joke.

To W. H. Auden, who first saw these

I hear the cries of evening, while the paw
Of dark, creeps up the turf:
Sheep bleating, swaying gull's cry, the rook's 'Caw',
The hammering surf.

I am inconstant, yet this constancy
Of natural rest, pulls at my heart;
Town-bred, I feel the roots of each earth-cry
Tear me apart.

These are the creakings of the dusty day
When the dog Night bites sharp,
These fingers grip my soul and tear away
And pluck me like a harp.

I feel the huge sphere turn, the great wheel sing
While beasts move to their ease:
Sheep's love, gull's peace—I feel my chattering
Uncared by these.

THE SWAN

The trumpets were curled away, the drum beat no more,
Only the Swan, the Swan, danced in my brain:
All night she spun; dropped, lifted again,
Arched and curved her arms; sunk on the frore
Snow-brittle feathers skirting her; reclined on hands
Buckling her waist, where the moon glanced.
How small her waist was, and the feet that danced!

Sometimes she bent back, and a breeze fanned
Her hair that touched the ground, and, shown
Between her Swan's legs, feathers and white down.

THAT GIRL WHO LAUGHED

That girl who laughed and had black eyes
Spoke here ten days ago. She smiles
Still in my thought; the lip still promises
The body lives, and the quick eye beguiles.

She lives beneath our common objects; dust
And chairs, and her few poems about the room.
Although death plays its tricks, and the earth's crust
Shallow her up in the enormous tomb,

I meet her every turn; the muffled part,
The stilled applause, the pageant to appall,
Startle her shade to take birth in my heart:
I see her dancing through the solid wall!

LYING AWAKE

Lying awake at night
      Shows again the difference
      Between me, and his innocence.
I vow he was born of light
      And that dark gradually
      Closed each eye,
He woke, he sleeps, so naturally.

So, born of nature, amongst humans divine,
He copied, and was, our sun.
      His mood was thunder
      For anger,
But mostly a calm, English one.

After Rilke: **O R P H E U S   E U R Y D I C E   H E R M E S**

That was the singular mine of souls.
Like still silver ores they went
As veins travelling its dark. Between roots
was the source of the blood that goes forth to men,
and heavy like porphyry it seemed in the dark.
Further, nothing red.

Rocks were there
and unreal woods. Bridges over voids
and yonder huge, grey, blind loch,
that over its far background hung
like rainy skies above a landscape.
And between meadows, of mild and full forbearance,
appeared the pale strip of the single road
laid in like a long pallor.

And on this single road they came.

Foremost the slender man in the blue mantle,
who stared in front of him, dumb and impatient.
Without chewing, his pace devoured the way
in great bites: his hands hung
heavy and clenched, out of the fall of folds.
And nothing more they knew of the light lyre,

which in the left had grown ingrown
like rose-tendrils in the olive tree bough.
And his senses were as if in two:
for whilst his glance ran before him like a dog,
turned round, went back and then away again
and waiting at the next corner stood—
his hearing hung back like an odour.
Sometimes it seemed to him as if it stretched
right to the walking of those other two,
who were to follow this whole climb.
At other times it was his climbing echo
only, and his mantle's draught, that were behind him.
He told himself, however, they'd surely come:
said it aloud, and heard his voice die away.
Indeed they'd come, only they were two
of terribly light going. Were he allowed
but once to turn (was not the looking back
sure dissolution of this entire labour,
now only being completed) he must see them,
the two soft-treading, who silently follow him:
the god of journeys and of far embassy,
with travelling cap over fair eyes,
carrying the slender rod before his body
and with wings fluttering at his ankles;
and given to his left hand—she.
She who was so much loved, that from a lyre
more lament came than from lamenting women:
and from lament a world was born, in which
all was recreated: wood and valley,
road, habitation, field and river and beast;

so that around this world of lament, just as
around the other earth a sun
and a star-set silent heaven went,
a heaven lamenting with distorted stars:—
this one who was so much loved.

And still she walked, leaning on that god's hand,
her step narrowed by the long winding sheet,
uncertain, mild and without impatience.
She was closed in herself, like one with child,
and thought not of the man who went before her,
nor of the road, which climbed up into life.
She was shut in herself. Her being dead
filled her like fullness.
Like a fruit with sweetness and the dark
so was she full with her great death,
which still remained so new, that she grasped nothing.

She was in a new maidenhood, and
untouchable; her sex was closed
like a young flower towards the evening
and now her hands to marriage were
so much estranged, that even the light god's
endlessly gentle guiding touch
offended her like a too great intimacy.

She had already ceased to be that woman,
the blonde who echoed through the poet's songs,
no more was she the great bed's scent and island
and that man's property no more.

She was already loosened like long hair,
abandoned like the fallen rain
and portioned out like hundredfold provision.
She was already root
when precipitately
the god did stop her and with pain in his call
the words spoke: 'He has turned'—
she grasped nothing and whispered softly: 'Who?'
But far off, dark before the light way out,
someone stood, whose countenance
could not be recognized. He stood and saw
how along the strip of meadow path
with mournful glance the god of embassy
silently turned, following the figure
already walking back on this same road,
her step narrowed by the long winding sheet,
uncertain, mild and without impatience.

(1935)